Decorative Wood Inlay

Decorative Wood Inlay

Zachary Taylor

The Crowood Press

First Published in 1997 by
The Crowood Press Ltd
Ramsbury, Marlborough
Wiltshire SN8 2HR

British Library Cataloguing-in-Publication Data
A catalogue reference for this book is available from the British Library

ISBN 1 86126 043 1

Line illustrations by David Fisher.

Acknowledgements
The author thanks the following for the supply of machines, equipment and
materials for the use in this book: William Adams, Tunbridge-ware;
Microflame Ltd (for Dremel products); Stewart MacDonald's Guitar Shop
Supply; J. Crispin and Sons; Carl Holtey; Veritas Woodworking Tools.
     Thanks also to Jane Julier for permission to use photographs of her work.
Cathy Challinor and Derek Basham kindly allowed their hands and work to be
used to illustrate purfling and rosette laying.

Photographic Acknowledgements
Andrew Crawford supplied photographs of his own work.
All other photography by the author.

Behold and rejoice ye Brethren of the Keyboard!
For the text was lost to its creator but was found again
by his computer counsellor and son-in-law
Christopher Isotta
to whom this book is affectionately dedicated.

Typefaces used: text, New Baskerville and Garamond; headings, Optima Bold.

Typeset and designed by
D & N Publishing
Membury Business Park, Lambourn Woodlands
Hungerford, Berkshire.

Printed and bound by Paramount Printing Ltd, Hong Kong.

Contents

Preface 6

1 INTRODUCTION: A BRIEF HISTORY OF THE CRAFT 9

2 TOOLS AND EQUIPMENT 13

3 THE IDEAL WORKSHOP 27

4 GROUNDS SUITABLE FOR RECEIVING INLAY .33

5 TYPES OF INLAY 35

6 SHARPENING 43

7 THE HOLTEY CUTTING GAUGE 55

8 INLAYING CORNER BANDING (FIRST METHOD) 57

9 INLAYING CORNER BANDING (SECOND METHOD) 61

10 INLAYING CORNER BANDING (THIRD METHOD)
   AND STRINGING (FIRST METHOD) 65

11 INLAYING STRINGING (SECOND METHOD) 69

12 INLAYING STRINGING (THIRD METHOD) 73

13 INLAYING CURVED STRINGING 77

14 PRINCIPLES OF EXCAVATION FOR INLAID MOTIFS 81

15 INLAYING MOTIFS OF CURVED OR IRREGULAR SHAPES 89

16 INLAYING A MOTIF AND LINE COMBINATION .93

17 INLAYING A ROSETTE 101

18 INLAYING PURFLING 105

19 CREATING AN INLAY TO FIT AN EXISTING RECESS 113

20 ADHESIVES 121

21 THE FINISH 122

Glossary 123

Index 126

Preface

It is not difficult to find manuals of instruction that commence with a section entitled 'Quick Start', most often printed in the early pages of tutorials that accompany computer software and the like. But do not labour under the illusion that abbreviated instruction is new. Although not part of a chapter suggesting that rapid assimilation was possible, in the 1903 edition of *The Handyman's Book* there appears an instruction on the inlaying of stringing:

If the shelves are to be inlaid, prepare a scratch tool of suitable width and run it round the edge as far as the design permits, finishing the remainder, after it has been set out, with chisels or gouges as may be most convenient.

I suggest it would have been 'most convenient' to have received more information – or, were the craftsmen of yesteryear so experienced that the author, Paul N. Hasluck, needed to express no more than this brief reference to the technique?

Well, there you have it; perhaps, Dear Reader, having read thus far and assimilated Mr Hasluck's instructions, you will have no need to waste any more time reading the rest of this book? Maybe if you have browsed your way through this introduction whilst standing at the shelf in the bookshop, you may now consider it unnecessary to purchase a copy of your own?

I am inclined to feel, however, that if the title attracted you enough to thumb apart its covers, the likelihood is that you have formed the distinct impression that there is somewhat more to the subject than may be contained in a few dozen words.

There must be a good reason for you to have selected this book, apart from its handsome cover and intriguing title. It could be that inlaid wood has become especially captivating to you and you have become urged to seek more information about the subject. Perhaps you have been attracted by the decoration of an item of furniture with an inlaid frondose motif brightening its otherwise plain surface? Or maybe you have come across a fine old violin with breathtaking purfling distinguishing its periphery? Maybe a handsome old writing slope has intrigued you with its banded corners in ebony and sycamore contrasting with its mahogany top?

It is important to define what is meant by 'inlaying'. Perhaps it is appropriate to point out what it isn't, to help to distinguish it from its related crafts. It isn't marquetry, in which shapes are cut from veneers and laid, with their edges touching, onto a ground to create a pictorial or decorative effect. It isn't parquetry, usually used to cover large areas, such as floors, where solid blocks are cut from contrasting woods and arranged in repetitive geometric patterns. Nor is it intarsia, that, in contemporary terms, has come to mean an application involving something of each of the two foregoing techniques; this method uses the edge-matching principles of marquetry but with material of sufficient thickness to permit contouring with low-relief carving.

Inlaying is the craft of inserting a motif or object into a corresponding recess.

Fig. 1 A selection of some of the test pieces used in this book.

Whether the recess is excavated to accept a prepared motif, or the motif is shaped to fill an existing recess, although differing in procedure, the essential requirement is to create as perfect a match as possible between the two parts. Without enlightenment there is mystery and whilst some of the most impressive inlaid decoration may appear to have been created by a genius, it is generally the result of straightforward craftsmanship, if the techniques are revealed.

Earth's last renewable resource, wood, with its seemingly immeasurable service to man, combines the properties of beauty and function. This unique material is the vehicle that links the designer, the artist, the craftsman and the admirer.

Combine these ingredients appropriately and mankind's relationship with nature is expressed in a most sublime way.

Some of the inlay craftsman's most satisfying moments will have been spent in the practice of inlaying wood, an experience that is partially renewed each time the decorated article is brought out and displayed for appreciation, by either an initiate or a master.

Make no mistake, this form of adornment at its tasteful best belongs to the past. Its ancient origins are set in a time when such things were not only greatly prized, but were being produced by abundant artisans; now, alas, reduced to a number likely to induce their categorization as an endangered species.

Yet – hold hard! The techniques are known, to those preservers of precious practices who value the wholesome pleasure of creating, for themselves, this special ornamentation.

As your guide to the subject, I have set out in this book various techniques accumulated during a third of a century of devoted study of woodwork, and they are intended to be of helpful inspiration, rather than a rigid, definitive, method. Great therapeutic benefits lie in wait for those whose lives are increasingly dominated by the pursuit of speed, if they indulge themselves in the study of this subject, where sufficient patient time must be set aside to accomplish, gently, the essential and pleasant tasks it demands.

So, instead of looking wistfully at the artefacts of yesteryear, convert the nostalgia into inspiration and speculate on the prospect of making some contribution to the enrichment of the future with your own skills. It is after all, part of our heritage, and not a barrier. A willing newcomer to the craft may aspire to similar heights of achievement, given enthusiasm for the subject, a little spare time, (oh, yes – and this book!)

I wish you great success and boundless joy from your endeavours, together with the hope that my book helps you attain them.

Zachary Taylor

1

Introduction: a Brief History of the Craft

As one might expect, the Egyptians did it thousands of years ago. The practice of ornamenting domestic artefacts and furniture with wood and precious materials is evidenced by the enormous amount of examples discovered in the tombs of the Pharaohs.

Admittedly, many of the adorned objects are more regal than commonplace, but simple stools and boxes with inlaid woods and ivory are as much in evidence as thrones and royal beds. Considering the Egyptians' lack of steel for tools to enable precise cutting of inlays and recesses, the delicate work bears witness to the great patience and ingenuity of the ancient craftsmen. Flint and copper were the principal materials used for the tools of those ancient carpenters and other woodworkers. Imagine how much time was taken in resharpening the teeth on a copper saw?

The Dark Ages were illuminated to an extent by Byzantine monastic orders, who

Fig. 2 A typical box from the Fourth Kingdom, Egypt, inlaid with ebony and ivory. British Museum, London.

Fig. 3 Shoulder knife used for creating recesses.

decorated their ecclesiastical furniture with wood mosaics, originals of which may be found throughout Northern Italy. Mosaic artforms were abandoned by the monks of the Gothic period, in favour of a technique using a 'shoulder-knife', with which they gouged out recesses for inlaying. A pictorial element began to appear at this time, depicting realistic images following the principles of painting, using wood, natural and artificially coloured, to create inlaid panels.

Since then, inlaying, along with its related crafts, has developed alongside other artforms, associated inevitably with furniture and other domestic paraphernalia.

A distinct advantage to the progressive development of inlaying in artistic terms, during the Renaissance era, was the involvement of the Italian craftsmen who were established artists in areas not necessarily associated directly with inlaying. As painters, sculptors and architects, they brought new dimensions to the subject, producing work that has rarely – some may say never – been improved upon. Having ventured into the dangerous subjective territory of 'art', there is no question that there are copious examples of work that ooze with consummate technique, but lack any evidence of artistry. It is equally obvious that the acknowledged work produced by the great masters would not have been possible without first having been the subject of carefully managed practical study. It should also be borne in mind that where technique is allowed to dominate, art is in danger of declining. Better for those without the ability to create artistically to rely on those who have, by honest copying, or at least referring unashamedly to some acknowledged great work for inspiration. Sometimes, it seems, those with the least ability in this respect are also those least aware of it, but that is another matter...

With the coming of machine saws in the sixteenth century, there was increased availability of veneers of consistent and controllable thickness. This meant that designs could be repeatable and, up to a point, such things as tools and equipment could be developed along standard lines to deal with the more dependable raw materials.

Recently, special machines have been used to peel veneers as thin as postcard from logs. This involves the prerequisite of preparing from the tree, a bark-free cylinder that is then supported horizontally on a type of lathe, reminiscent of a giant mother-of-all pencil-sharpeners! As the log revolves, a cutting edge is forced against it that effectively unwinds a continuous ribbon of veneer, producing hundreds of metres of material, reducing the core diameter to little more than the thickness of a man's wrist.

As to the progress of inlaid work, there can be little doubt that the making of musical instruments – or, to use its more erudite term, lutherie – has contributed more than its fair share. From the very earliest times to the present day, stringed instruments have been treated as viable vehicles for inlay, from simple rebecs bearing modest statements using geometric patterns, up to the breathtaking German barytons adorned with exquisitely worked Arcadian scenes and all variations between.

Furniture and cabinetwork has also been treated to ornamentation by inlay of a very wide variety. With the exception of the plain appearance of nineteenth century Shaker furniture, almost all eras have contributed to the development of some type of inlaid decoration. Whether one looks at the inlay of panels of the Tunbridge-ware type, in themselves a form of mosaic, or the delicate marquetry motifs produced in quantity since the eighteenth century to ornament boxes, table tops and other articles, they play their part in elevating the plain to the picturesque.

Today's inlaying is found mostly in reproduction pieces, humbly copying the examples of our craftsman forebears; modern pieces bearing inlaid decoration occur less frequently. Why? Let us not assume that the current trend to 'simplify' and 'minimalize' is always a reverent seeking for contemporary aesthetic expression. Very often it is evidence of commercial pressures generated by the need to supply cheaper goods. The faster the rate of production, the cheaper it is to produce. I inspected a complete office suite recently, made almost entirely of folded cardboard! The received wisdom of our knowledgeable mentors is that there is no longer room in our world for fancy, outdated, decoration. Well, maybe there is, and maybe it need not be outdated. Anyway, who says what the current trends should be? You may wager confidently, if anybody has a hand on that particular steering wheel, it is

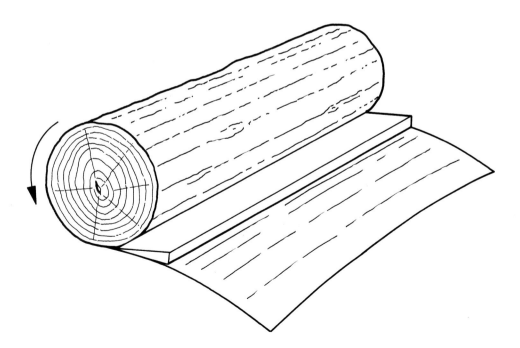

Fig. 4 A diagrammatic view of a rotary veneer-cutter, showing a blade peeling a continuous sheet of veneer from a rotating log.

Fig. 5 A fine example of inlaid motifs and marquetry in a French nineteenth-century secretaire. This may be seen along with many other similar pieces at the British Museum, London.

the management of high-powered manufacturing systems out for profit from the gullible consumer at the cost of all else.

A general lack of textbooks on the subject and the loss of hand-me-down techniques due to lack of continuity has meant the need for some fresh approaches in methodology, perhaps resulting in some alternative approaches. But, as long as the end results are of matching quality, it matters little if technical application differs, either from craftsman to craftsman, or age to age.

2

Tools and Equipment

Tools fall into two basic categories; those used for excavating recesses and those for shaping inlays.

TOOLS FOR EXCAVATING RECESSES

CHISELS AND GOUGES

Chisels are for stabbing cuts to define edges and ends of recesses, for trimming joints in stringing and for excavating floors of recesses. Gouges in small sizes, are of various shapes to clear away waste material from the bottom faces of recesses. These are generally more suitable if of the spoon and fish-tail combination.

TOOTHPICK CHISEL

Made from a standard 50mm (2in) oval nail, bent after insertion into a wooden handle and shaped on a grindstone to

Fig. 6 A selection of chisels and gouges suitable for recessing and trimming.

(Left) *Fig. 7 An oval nail inserted into a wooden handle and bent about 60 degrees.*

(Above) *Fig. 8 The head of the nail has been shaped on a bench grinder.*

form a chisel point. It could be done with a file just as effectively. Used to remove waste from narrow channels and to clean out corners. It is useful to have a small selection of widths and end shapes to cope with various contingencies.

PURFLING CUTTER

Something of a misnomer, in that the purfling cutter is generally used to mark, define and cut the channels to receive purfling, rather than the purfling itself. It could be used, however, for the cutting of purfling, but normally such inlays are purchased from specialist suppliers. The one depicted here is made by Carl Holtey. Its intended function is detailed in Chapter 18.

KNIFE

Scalpel and craft types are used for deepening edge-cuts and general trimming of peripheral forms. Craft knives of the type with blades that slide into handles are not suitable, owing to the lack of rigidity in the blade fitting. The instability of the design renders the knife prone to wandering. Customized knives are available with smooth, bevel-less sides for marking around motifs.

*Fig. 9 This is a refined example of a purfling cutter made by
Carl Holtey to the author's specification. The handle is Brazilian
rosewood and the metals are stainless steel and gunmetal.*

*Fig. 10 Knives used in marking, trimming and incising. The first
two from the left were made from cut-throat razors by the author.*

If a regular cabinet maker's marking knife is used, and I refer to the short-bladed knife with a bevel on only one side, i.e., the right side bevelled for a right-handed person, it will be inadequate for our purpose in this instance. Our needs are for faithful transference of the shape of the motif onto the ground. This means that a blade with a single bevel will present a different bearing surface on opposite sides and therefore requires dissimilar application. To avoid this problem use a knife with identical bevels on either side of the cutting edge.

Special adaptations are made to hold two blades separated by shims to make double cutters for channelling. The 'odd-leg' dividers detailed below are a derivation of this, but superior, since they are adjustable to suit the purfling width.

CIRCLE-CUTTER

Made especially for the edge-cutting of circles for the inlay of rosettes and other circular motifs. It may be used also for the cutting out of motifs for inlaying. Various models are available, differing in levels of sophistication. The less gadget-ridden, the easier they are to handle, as a general rule. As with all cutting tools, most work well, provided the blades are properly sharpened.

HAND-ROUTER

Sometimes called, rather rudely, an 'old-woman's tooth', the hand-router is a small single cutter held in a frame for excavating a fixed and predetermined depth. As with the circle-cutter and related tools, the less complex, the less trouble. Being bent at

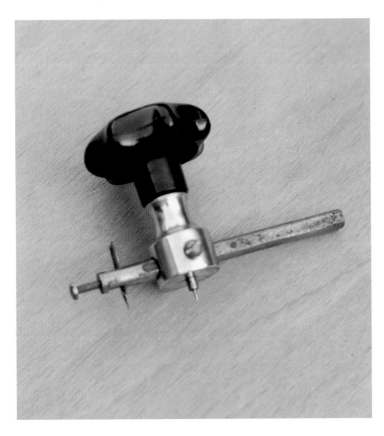

Fig. 11 Circle-cutter for incising circles prior to excavating channels, or for cutting circular motifs. The blade is a piece of broken file, ground to suit and sharpened to a razor edge.

Fig. 12 Two sizes of hand-router. On the left is the common size for most inlay work; the other is for wide grooving and setting down large areas.

right angles, the blade is tricky to sharpen as it is difficult to hold whilst honing, but perseverance pays dividends.

SCRATCH-STOCK

Scratch-stocks are of various, and customized forms, to hold shaped blades. They are applied to edges in a scraping motion to remove waste of a given depth and width. The one shown is one of the easiest to make, since it need consist only of scraps of wood and an old hacksaw blade. It was made in a few minutes about twenty years ago.

SCRAPER

Of the cabinet-maker's type or the two-handed Stanley variety, for cleaning back inlays and removing superfluous material to create a smooth surface. The uninitiated may find the blade something of a mystery. Advice on sharpening and the use of the 'ticketer' will be found in Chapter 6.

The two-handed scraper, sometimes called a scraper-plane, has the advantage of making surfaces level as well as smooth. Somewhat tricky to set up, but they are superb tools when the burred edge and blade exposure are balanced correctly.

Fig. 13 An old hand-made scratch-stock made from a piece of much-used elm, proving again that where wood is concerned, there is no such thing as 'scrap'! A piece of broken hacksaw blade and a wingnut and bolt are all that is necessary to make up this simple but effective tool.

Fig. 14 A two-handed scraper by Stanley (top), a flexible cabinet-maker's scraper (bottom left) and a heavier more rigid type (bottom right).

PLANE

Any size of smoothing plane may be used for surface levelling and general smoothing prior to the embedding process. The one shown was made by Carl Holtey, now highly respected for his Norris replicas. It would be fair to say that Carl does not create true copies of the Norris plane, his being superior in finish and function. The thumb plane was made to the author's requirement with a low angle, extra hard blade and a very narrow throat to ensure a clean slice with reduced risk of tearing out grain.

SCRAPER-PLANE

A special tool designed and made by the author, to scrape and level simultaneously

Fig. 15 A thumb plane by Carl Holtey to the author's requirements, based on a Norris pattern.

Fig. 16 A faithful elderly tool designed and made by the author.

up to 100mm (4in) wide. It is easily made by an experienced woodworker.

After setting the blade level with the work surface, cut is increased by turning the adjusting screw that bears on the blade deflector causing the blade to bow. Sharpening scraper blades is detailed in Chapter 6.

MOTORIZED ROUTER

The electric router is one of the most common machine tools found in the contemporary workshop – that is hardly surprising, since it is one of the most versatile tools a woodworker may own, with applications for an inlayer, too.

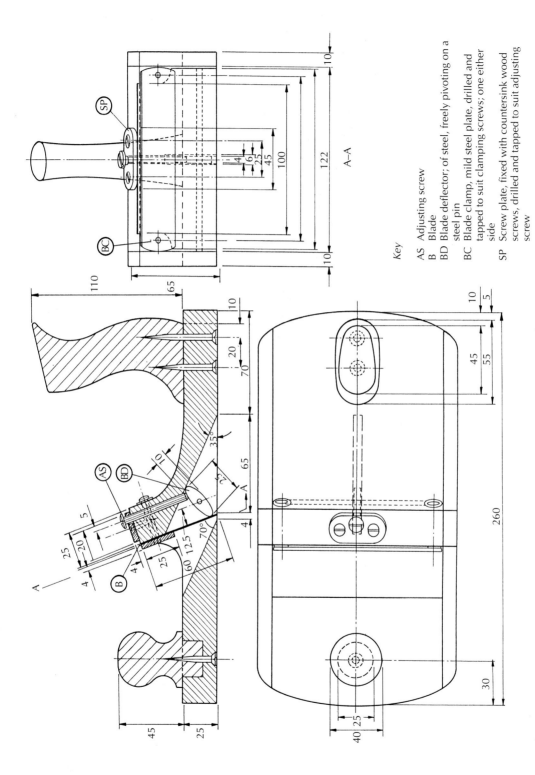

Fig. 17 Scraper plane adapted and made by the author from a design in Robert Wearing's inspiring book, Woodworking Aids and Devices.

One of the smaller varieties such as the Dremel Multi Model 395 is ideal for our purposes, as many useful and appropriate accessories are available to extend its range of application. A router attachment and a router table are available from the manufacturer and there are other compatible items including specially developed accessories for inlaying from suppliers such as Stewart MacDonald. Several are demonstrated in this book.

BRUSHES

Use simple, soft, short-bristle brushes to remove debris from the channels and recesses during and after completion of the excavation. The type which is available for camera care and which incorporates a puffer is handy.

(Above) *Fig. 18 Dremel Multi Model 395 with its router attachment. Speeds from 10,000 to 37,000 r.p.m. drive rotary cutters for a wide variety of applications.*

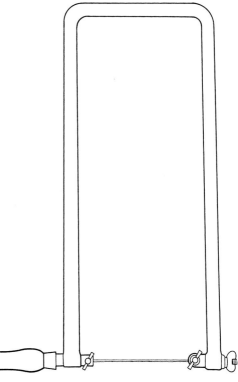

Fig. 19 A hand-operated fretsaw used for cutting out motifs.

Fig. 20 This is a typical powered scrollsaw. Incorporated features may include a tilting table, dust blower, quick-release blade holders and variable speeds.

TOOLS FOR SHAPING INLAYS

SAWS

Most people will master the hand-held fretsaw quickly enough to produce intricate motifs from thin wood. Standard saw blades are available internationally, in various specifications, but generally inlay work demands fine-toothed types. A home-made 'keyhole' table that can be fitted temporarily to the work-top makes life much easier when sawing small motifs and the like. *See* Chapter 18 for more information.

A modern alternative to the hand-powered fretsaw is the motorized scrollsaw, many versions of which are available, allowing a 'both hands on' contact with the workpiece as the blade reciprocates vertically. Production of inlay motifs is possible in a wide variety of materials.

The book *Success with the Scrollsaw* by the author of this book, published by The Crowood Press, lists many models and teaches essential techniques using exemplary projects.

ODD-LEG DIVIDERS

So-called, because the ends of the two legs of the callipers, normally of equal length, are unequal. One leg is shortened to run along a surface, creating an incision parallel to a previously incised line in which the longer leg is tracking. Both legs are ground to a sharp point and knife-edged to permit a cutting action. The width is adjusted by rotation of the thumbscrew and since the circular hinge is of spring steel. the legs are held securely in position. Its use is detailed in Chapter 18.

STRINGING-THICKNESSER

A purpose-made tool for regulating the thickness of stringing or any piece of wood up to about 6mm (¼in) thick and about 50mm (2in) wide. The one shown in use here was given to the author by Bob Wearing, a craftsman/author/journalist and designer of many superb devices.

Let us call this process 'thicknessing', for want of a term. It is a simple matter to reduce the thickness and smooth the surface of the inlay by passing it between the blade and the

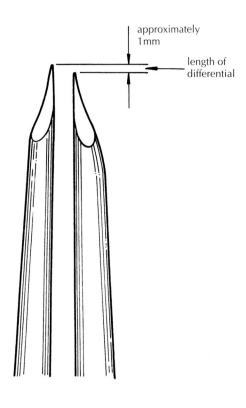

approximately
1mm

length of
differential

(Above) *Fig. 21 A standard pair of engineer's dividers adapted by re-forming the points by grinding. One leg is shorter than the other, but both legs have knife blade points to perform as incisors.*

(Above right) *Fig. 22 Showing the legs of unequal length, typical of odd-leg dividers. They are used for scribing a second line parallel to an existing one by inserting the longer leg into the incision and using the shorter one to mark the second line.*

Fig. 23 Thicknesser in use, showing a strip of string being fed through the gap between the blade and the table.

(Above) *Fig. 24 Stringing is fed through several times, gradually reducing in thickness as it is passed through and across the table. The gap is smaller on one side to permit a fine graduation of the process.*

Fig. 25 Three metal components make up the thicknesser; a cast base plus the blade and top iron from a spokeshave. The blade edge is relieved at each corner to avoid tramlines and it is set to give a slight angled gap above the table, to permit gradual thicknessing of the string.

table of the thicknesser. Since the blade is similar to a spokeshave but set up with the cutting edge away from the feed of the workpiece, it follows that the inlay is forced against the back of the blade to remove waste by a scraping action. The blade is set to create a greater gap on one side and at a height to admit the stringing in a raw sawn state. As the inlay is drawn past the blade in order to remove the waste, gradually it is traversed across progressively with each pass towards the side with the smaller gap set to the required finished height. Adjustment of the thicknesser is available via the screw guides. A few passes should ensure a perfectly level and smooth string of uniform thickness throughout its length.

OTHER TOOLS

Ancillary to the tools required for recessing or the direct cutting of the component parts of the inlays, are the following:

STEEL STRAIGHT-EDGE

For marking, scoring and guiding of depth-cutting of straight channel walls.

(Right) *Fig. 26 A roller used for pressing down motifs. This type is available from art-suppliers as ink/paint rollers. Smaller ones are available for pressing wallpaper joints.*

SET-SQUARE

For marking right-angular references, laying out, etc.

SLIDING BEVEL

Intended to serve as a guide for marking and cutting angles.

SEAM-ROLLER

Of the type decorators use to apply pressure at seams and joints in wallpapering; it applies considerable force due to the point-loading of the roller contact.

VENEER HAMMER

Used for the application of local pressure on flat motifs or stringing, etc. This is another tool made readily by the inlayer from scrap materials.

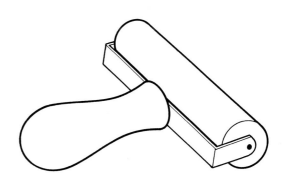

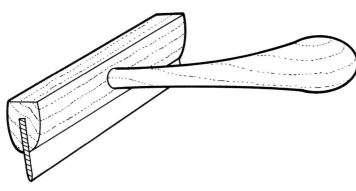

(Left) *Fig. 27 Often made from scraps, this veneer hammer has a metal tongue to give local pressure when applied to laying veneer or inlaid motifs.*

MARKING GAUGE

Marking gauges are not only for marking parallel lines, but if fitted with a knife-type blade are also useful for cutting initial guides prior to waste removal operations in conjunction with a scratch-stock, for instance. This will work well for cutting waste from recesses suitable for corner banding.

CLAMPS

Various clamps are needed for the securing of workpieces during recessing and inlaying. Remember to use some form of cushioning between the clamp faces and the workpiece to prevent bruising. Better still, glue facings of cork or similar material to the clamp jaws for immediate use without the need to find suitable material for buffering.

SHARPENING APPARATUS

Stones, hones and strops. More details are given later in the book.

MAGNIFYING LENS

For inspection of fine detail. The most practical are the twin-lens types that are fitted to a headband, leaving the hands free. Another variety is a lens supported on a stand, incorporating a light; these tend to take up bench-space, however, and seem always to be in the way.

Other items of equipment, such as benches and lighting, are referred to in the next chapter.

Fig. 28 Three types of gauge are shown: top left is a cutting gauge fitted with a knife-blade marker. The other two have points suitable for marking mortises and tenons, as well as rebates and the like.

— 3 —

The Ideal Workshop

Of course, the reader will realize that in specifying the ideal workshop, I am describing my idea of a place that has ample space, is well-lit, comfortable, warm, dry and fully equipped with every tool and piece of equipment necessary to hand and stored ready for use in its proper place. Throw in self-cleaning for good measure and it would probably take a fire to get me out of the place! Unless you are building the workshop from scratch, however, with adequate funds to equip the place as needed, some compromise will be necessary.

Some craftsmen, working from home, have no separate workshop set aside for their hobbies, and have to use a part of their home for such purposes. In the craft of inlaying, if the area of interest lies in the smaller range of projects, the amount of space required may be supplied by the kitchen table. Naturally, in such a case, it becomes necessary to pack away at the end of each practical session, demanding convenient and adequate storage for the toolkit and the work in progress. Nevertheless, this kind of situation might still be referred to as 'ideal' to some folk and, if managed carefully, may be adequate for the production of work equal in quality to the best.

THE WORK-BENCH

Speaking of the kitchen table, or workbench, this is one of the essentials requiring the application of fundamental principles. Apart from the need to provide a surface of sufficient size to accept the workpiece, and the necessary tooling with which it will be associated at any one time, it must be stable and at the correct height.

Presumably, due to the length of time involved in the practice of inlaying, noted more for its leisurely pace than for either its rapidity, or high volume production, most people would prefer to be seated at the workplace. It follows that, in general, for this kind of application, the work-top is best at a height equivalent to the elbow with the upper arms at the side of the body and the forearms horizontal; there is clearly a dimensional relationship between the work-top and the chair. My own preference is for a relatively high bench, sufficient for comfortable work when standing, i.e., an old fashioned yard – approximately 915mm. With a stool at about 26in plus a cushion (about 1in thick when compressed) (about 590mm plus 25mm respectively) this brings about an ergonomically convenient disposition for my work. It equates to a seat-to-bench-top differential of 9in (220mm). Some simple experiments should be undertaken to verify the most suitable relationship between these two essentials, for the sake of comfort and physical application. Without these two factors adjusted to produce their optimum benefit, efficiency and precision will quickly deteriorate.

As to the stability of the work-bench: all efforts to prevent rocking must be exercised. Most four-legged pieces of furniture are potential rockers, due to unequal legs or irregularities in the floor surface on which they stand – maybe both. This is one of the reasons why many stands designed for use with small machines are three-legged, like milking stools, although the splay of the legs and their size relative to the size of the table is crucial.

Shown in Fig. 29 and in many other illustrations too, is the Veritas bench, incorporating various significant features, among which are the much-used bench dogs. These may be seen holding the workpieces clamped to the bench-top whilst various processes are being carried out. The principle of 'dog' clamping is simple and effective. Holes are drilled in the bench top and in the edges of the wooden-faced vice jaws. The holes are for the location of dogs that are used as clamps, one or more fixed in the bench top, one or more in the movable vice, permitting a clamping action. The so-called 'Wonder dog' uses a similar principle as a vice or clamp, being adjustable with a screw thread, and this may be located by its pillar in any of the bench-top holes. If the dogs project above the workpiece it is an easy matter to use a packing piece next to the clamp to avoid collisions with recessing tools.

Providing the bench or table can be fixed in one spot, then discrepancies may be corrected by strategic wedging against the floor; usually just one leg needs the correction.

Bracketing the bottom of the legs for subsequent bolting to the floor is advantageous if it can be arranged. A flap-table, hinged against the wall can be very effective in this respect, being stable due to the wall anchorage and easily levelled with only one or two legs to support the free end. This type of work-bench, featuring a fold-away facility, has its own particular appeal to those whose home-life and hobbies take place in close proximity. Some proprietary brands have recently appeared on the market, but most people could manage to construct one from basic boards and hardware.

A bench-top needs to be flat and inflexible. Some might read this as meaning a metal construction is necessary. This would undoubtedly work; however, as with other categories of woodwork, wood is more

Fig. 29 A favourite bench, made by the author from Veritas parts, including the bench dogs, Wonder dogs and hold-down. A side-vice and a twin-screw end-vice complete the ensemble. The top is made from maple, the side rails and base from walnut.

appropriate for working surfaces. It is obviously compatible with the material used for inlaying and it is more pleasant to the touch than metal, as well as being kinder to blades and other cutting implements that will come into contact with it.

Notwithstanding the aesthetics of a natural wooden top, the material that is used must be able to withstand some hard knocks and must resist bending. So, not too soft a wood, and if less than 25mm (1in), it should be supported with battens to stiffen it. It should not be necessary to varnish or polish the surface – this would quickly become scratched and unsightly.

Alternatives to solid timber are laminated boards, plywood, blockboard and other veneered panels, but these, whilst stable and less prone to warping, have the disadvantage of suffering delamination of the exterior surface due to honest wear. Many may shrink from my suggestion to use MDF (medium density fibreboard), but as a work-top it represents a flat, smooth, durable, inexpensive surface, easily managed. If appearances are important, (and they should be, to a craftsman with aspirations to artistic inlay projects) a wooden framing can be added to the edge of the MDF to enhance its appearance.

A final word about stools; if acquiring a seat, try a swivelling, height-adjustable, upholstered, typist's or draughtsman's chair. These are relatively cheap and a second-hand one is good enough for a workshop situation; these are available by the truckload from dealers in used office furniture. Many have rollers to permit ease of relocation, but these do not lend themselves to the stability required for precision work at the bench.

LIGHTING

Natural light from an overhead source, such as a north-facing roof-light, is preferable, being consistent and without the tendency

Fig. 31 Over the bench are three spotlights and two halogen spots. All are on universal brackets for precise localized illumination. A floor-standing model (in black) and an illuminated lens (in white) make up a comprehensive lighting kit. At the farthest point from the camera can be seen the steel cabinet used for storage of flammable and other potentially dangerous substances.

Fig. 30 A sturdy swivelling stool, adjustable for height and back-rest angle. It is best without floor-rollers, for stability.

to cast strong shadow. This, however, suffers from the obvious disadvantage of availability, since it limits the worker to day-time use. A less obvious disadvantage is that it doesn't throw a directional shadow when this is required. This point will be examined later in the book in the context of inspection of flat, finished, surfaces.

So, even if a top-light is available, some supplementary illumination will be necessary. Fluorescent tubes are acceptable for general lighting, although many folk dislike them for various reasons – humming, flicker, a 'flat' feel about the light-spread. Tungsten or halogen bulbs are better and these are available in small spot-lamps, eminently suitable for close work where space may be restricted.

HEATING

In a situation where woods, delicate and precious, are the basic raw materials concerned, heating along with other environmental factors is of prime consideration.

Of the various forms of heating, some dry out the atmosphere while others fill it with moisture. Humidity is not easy to control but to some extent, steps can be taken to balance this. If a branch of the domestic central heating system can be brought into the workshop, fine, but this usually has the effect of drying out not only the air but everything else within the enclosed space – ask any piano-tuner. Paraffin or other oil-burning appliances load the atmosphere with unbelievable moisture content, and without a sophisticated humidity control system many ill-effects may ensue. The same applies to gas-burning heaters.

Follow this to its logical conclusion and our enthusiast will move the workshop into a modern hotel bedroom with air-conditioning! But, wait. A thermostatically-controlled electric oil-filled radiator, with a water-container attached, is probably the simplest compromise. Sufficient heat should be forthcoming from the heater to maintain a prescribed temperature for working comfort, whilst supplying water by absorption back into the atmosphere at the same rate at which it is being dried out. Ventilation, permitting a free-flowing supply from a natural source will also help.

It is probably unnecessary to state the dangers of heat in close proximity to the work area. Any direct heat has the potential to change the shape of wood in any form, not necessarily permanently but usually inconveniently.

MACHINERY

This may include machines to drive abrasive discs and belts, power drills, motorized scrollsaws, electric routers and flexible drives. Only two of these items are mentioned in the list of tools and equipment (*see* Chapter 2); that is the router and the scrollsaw. Perhaps this indicates that the rest are non-essential; so no need to go to the trouble of acquiring them. If they are already owned, like as not the owner will already be sufficiently familiar with their operation.

Even so, a word about the general topic. Being of a portable category, the above machines are best stored during downtime, to avoid clutter, unless they are used often enough to dedicate to them permanent work-space.

Powered abrasives such as disc- or belt-sanders can be useful where large panels are involved, but even so, taking into consideration the payback in terms of productivity, it is doubtful if it warrants the investment, weight, noise, dust and storage.

A router at the smaller end of the range may be an asset for cutting channels for banding, with the proviso, if enough of this kind of work makes it worth while.

Motorized scrollsaws are excellent for the preparation of motifs, especially the variable speed models, that allow a slow speed of stroke for navigating tricky outlines in delicate materials.

If powered abrasives and routers are being used, then it is sensible to use some form of dust extraction during their operation. Many machines now feature extractor ports with adaptation to suit various nozzles including those fitted to domestic vacuum cleaners.

SAFETY AT WORK

An obvious link with the foregoing subjects of heating and machinery is that of safety, particularly of protection against fire. It is all too easy to leave this consideration till last, or even to ignore it altogether, because it won't happen, will it? And anyway it's a boring topic, isn't it? Maybe, but safety awareness is an essential ingredient in a complete workshop environment.

On the old principle that prevention is better than an insurance claim, ask the local fire-prevention officer for any advice on this subject, especially if there are unusual features pertaining to your situation. Consider first the highly inflammable nature of adhesives, polish, varnish, spirits of various kinds, all of which are likely to be needed from time to time. Add to this the stock of woods, paper, dusters and other associated items, and we have a potential fire bomb that would gladden the heart of any arsonist.

It is best to keep the flammable liquids in a steel cabinet or in a metal container within a cupboard, if the latter is of wood. When being used on the bench, these liquids should never be unstoppered except when transferring quantities into smaller vessels for application. The latter should be broad-based and, as far as possible, untippable. Fixing the container by tape to the bench top or to a supplementary base may increase security.

Fig. 32 If any inflammable or otherwise dangerous liquid needs to be open for any length of time, it is best to tape it down to the bench or a temporary base to reduce the risk of spillage.

Cloths, tissues and wire wool used for cleaning surfaces or mopping-up glues and polishes should be destroyed after use and not left in drawers or other enclosures. This avoids the risk of unscheduled combustion, possibly when the workshop is deserted. Such items are known to ignite spontaneously under appropriate conditions.

Chisels, gouges and knives are just as good at cutting flesh as wood. When not in use they are best protected by some sheath or cover; corks work well as a cover for the stabbing type of blade. Flexible plastic tubes are fine for containing chisels and gouges; better still if they are transparent.

STORAGE

As mentioned above, storage for flammable items and machinery must be a priority with safety in mind as well as convenience, but what of the rest of the kit? Small tools that are required frequently may be attached temporarily or even permanently to magnetic strips. A distinct advantage to the magnetic rack is that the tool kit can be varied from time to time according to the job in hand.

With the constant danger of rusting and other effects of oxidation to exposed metals, even in well-balanced environments, due to condensation, it is best to put away tools that may be prone to this kind of problem. Bearing in mind that the inlayer uses fewer tools than most woodworkers, and most of his kit is relatively small, it should not be difficult to devise an efficient storage system.

Drawers near or under the bench are usually handy – either a small chest that may stand at the side of the bench (with the slight disadvantage that access to the lower ones demand the operator to bend) or drawers attached to the underside of the bench-top.

Fig. 33 For handy temporary storage of tools needed for inlaying in progress, a rack fitted with magnetic strips is efficient. This may be designed to stand on the bench nearby, keeping the tools off the valuable work-space and always to hand.

Grounds Suitable for Receiving Inlay

TYPES OF GROUND

The term 'ground' refers to whatever is the material, or item, into which the inlay is to be inserted. The purpose of the inlay is primarily to enhance the appearance of the object, so its colour and texture must be pertinent to the ground, requiring co-ordination of the two elements together with their shapes and sizes.

Many types of ground are used and usually they are associated with a particular object, such as furniture or other artefact. Table tops, for instance, being generally one of the largest and probably plainest items of domestic furniture, are ideal subjects for

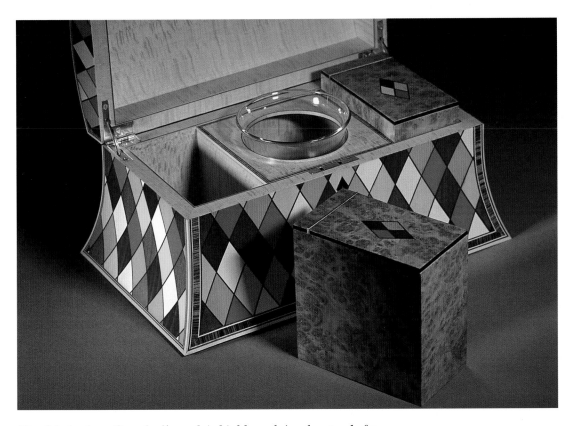

Fig. 34 Andrew Crawford's work is highly acclaimed not only for his fine craftsmanship but for his artistic treatment of materials associated with design and function.

Fig. 35 The boxes shown are examples of Andrew Crawford's creativity; evidence that a sensitive craftsman may combine traditional and contemporary elements to produce magnificent results.

decoration. Here are opportunities to inlay a central motif and a border string. Whether of one-piece solid construction or a framed panel variety, it serves much the same purpose from the inlayer's viewpoint. It would not matter if the top had been veneered; the inlaying technique need not be any different from the application to a solid top, except for the following caveat: normally, after insetting any inlaid decoration, it is necessary to clean back the surfaces to bring the components level and smooth. Clearly, there is a limit to how much cutting-back can be undertaken with a veneered top. With a standard veneer of say, 0.6mm, few liberties can be taken in this operation.

Writing slopes were sometimes treated to ornate decoration – some might feel they were somewhat over-expressed. Now and then, one sees an example constructed from excellent material with tasteful ornamentation. Maybe an oval motif on the lid, with a corner trimmed in a laminated banding of alternate ebony and sycamore. Like as not, the writing slope also carries fair specimens of inlaid metalwork, in the way of hinges and catches.

In this case, the material of the ground will almost certainly be solid hardwood – mahogany, perhaps – or if it is veneered, then the carcass will be made from one of the better-quality softwoods. Many modern workshops producing items such as these are using MDF for very good reasons. The material is easily worked, stable and inexpensive.

— 5 —

Types of Inlay

Inlaying associates two basic elements: the inlay, and the ground into which it will be embedded. Considering the inlaid component, material specification depends greatly upon which types of inlay are required; without exception, however, they are made from hardwoods. Exotic timbers of bright, dark, or otherwise spectacular hues are greatly prized, although dyes or stains are used to colour common pale hardwoods such as box or sycamore. Inlaid components may be called by any of the following (note, the first three names are often interchanged): banding, binding, stringing, lines, purfling, rosettes or motifs.

- **Banding, or binding**, is usually laid into a corner of a box or panel, with the dual function of decoration and protection. Hardwoods are the norm, and are often made of several laminations of veneer thickness.
- **Stringing**: often inset from the edge of a panel or frame, stringing is generally

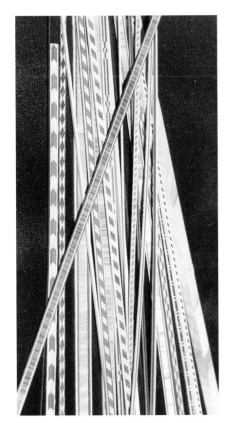

(Left) *Fig. 36 An assortment of corner binding, stringing and purfling, giving an idea of the range of colour and style in common use.*

(Right) *Fig. 37 Types of purfling. From top: plain banding, decorative stringing with patterned insert, plain line, two-colour purfling.*

35

Fig. 38 Usually produced for, not by, the luthier, rosettes are a special item in the inlayer's repertoire. Compare these with examples of 'Tunbridge-ware' exhibited in craft museums and the like.

straight and made up of several veneers embodying a pattern within its structure.

- **Lines**: as the name suggests, these are plain lines available usually in boxwood, rosewood and ebony, in widths from 1 to 6mm. Dyes are used to stain boxwood and other light woods.
- **Purfling**: a type of stringing, but produced for the musical-instrument maker, though other woodworkers use it. Normally three veneers thick; two dark outer layers enclosing a lighter-coloured inner.
- **Rosettes**: again, produced for the luthier, but not exclusively. Rosettes are seen most often as the decoration around a circular soundhole and comprising a composite of plain rings from lines or purfling for the outer and inner diametric elements, enclosing 'Tunbridge ware'-style mosaics.
- **Motifs**: many and various, not necessarily of a common geometric shape, i.e., oval or rectangular, but normally so. Sizes may be as small as 15mm (less than ⅝in) or over 300mm (12in). Background veneers are usually mahogany or walnut. These are available in quantity from veneer houses who specialize in pictorial and traditional subjects produced by marquetry specialists.

It is not unusual to combine two or more of the above types of inlay, to produce wider inlays, such as may be seen on the corner banding of guitars. Here there may be

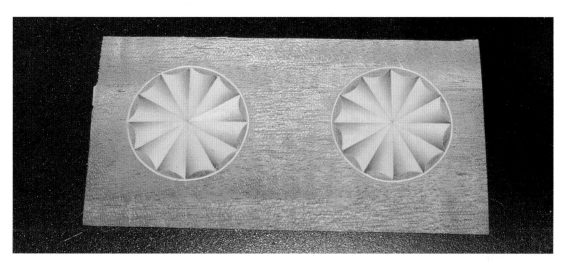

Fig. 39 Two circular motifs with shaded portions giving a three-dimensional effect. The technique is achieved by partial scorching, placing the area to be darkened into hot sand.

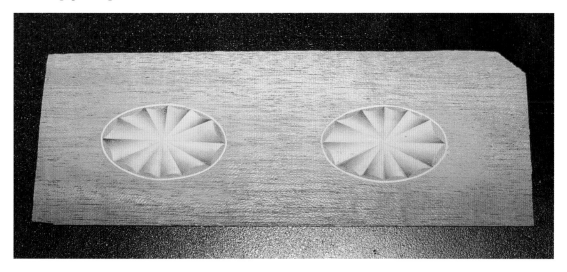

Fig. 40 Oval motifs made similarly to the circular ones above. A marquetry technique using a scrollsaw is used to produce this type of inlay.

found a three-veneer purfling enclosed by a plain banding. In some examples, the Maggini violin family for instance, double purfling is a hallmark. In this case, two lines of black/white/black purflings are inlaid, separated by a gap of a few millimetres.

Occasionally, it may be necessary to make up banding, lines, etc., using less standard materials, or unusual thickness, for special effects. For this purpose one may turn to the veneer suppliers for the necessary raw materials.

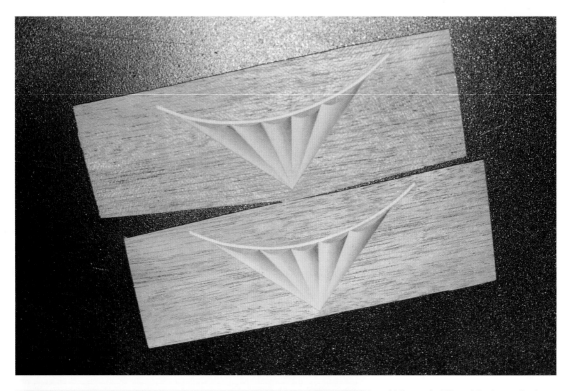

(Above) *Fig. 41 A variation on the theme of mock-shading enhances these corner designs.*

Fig. 42 Floral and shell symbols have been used for centuries in marquetry designs.

Fig. 43 Typical of traditional motifs is this composition of musical instruments using well-selected coloured woods.

Veneers come in a wide range of woods and grain-patterns. The latter depends on the manner of cutting and from where in the log it was cut. Sawn veneer is either quarter-sawn on radials from the log, or flat-cut from blocks and these have a different appearance from those sliced from the half-round or rotary-peeled.

From certain irregular outgrowths come burrs, found occasionally on the trunks of some species, like elm, oak, ash, walnut and other hardwoods. Veneers cut from these abnormalities give dramatic visual effects due to the swirling interlocked grain. Slices taken through crotches and roots produce curls and spectacular figure, prized for veneering tables and other large panels.

Consecutive slices are often placed side by side and edge-joined, to make what is known as 'book-matching', as if two consecutive pages were opened. This 'mirrors'

and thus emphasizes grain features. In the early part of this century most homes contained examples of this technique, adorning sideboards, wardrobes and the like. Colours available from the wood-colour spectrum are amazingly varied, from palest, such as holly, to black ebony, with reds, purples, oranges, greens, yellows plus occasional non-conformist timbers with colours that defy description. A piece of American black walnut I came across was almost black on one side of a plank and pink on the other, as if two unrelated species had been stuck together.

Colour plays an enormous part in the selection of the material for both inlay and ground. Usually, one of the two, either the inlay or the ground, has already been chosen for one reason or another and this will dictate the basis of the colour scheme. By the nature of 'woody' things, there will

Fig. 44 The sensitive shading and carefully chosen woods of this contemporary motif keep faith with its older relatives.

(Below) *Fig. 45 Greco-Roman symbols as depicted in this example were used frequently to decorate furniture from the seventeenth to the nineteenth centuries.*

generally be a predominance of brown, but within that colour range will be subdivisions of brown, yellow and red.

Some of the browns and yellows are compatible, say rosewood and yew, for example, but beware of mixing browns and reds. Walnut and mahogany clash resoundingly. Safer are the marriages between the very dark or the very pale with almost any other colour. Ebony or holly, to take the opposing terminals of the colour range, will work with almost any other colour, particularly striking if used together.

Woods coloured by dying extend the spectrum of wood colour to include virtually any hue or shade, and many well-respected inlay practitioners use them. My own preference is to use natural colours wherever possible, thus avoiding both the messy inconvenience of the colouring operation, or the frustration of tracking down odd pieces from commercial suppliers.

Where a musical instrument is concerned, depending on the era, almost any part of it may be decorated. Inlay is superior to say, paint, or other surface treatment, since durability to withstand handling is a necessary consideration. It is generally the stringed instrument family that is favoured for this work, being made essentially of wood, with fairly large areas that might otherwise be rather bland in appearance.

Fig. 46 Inlaid purfling around the edges, front and back, and a rosette adorn this guitar made by the author. It is built on classical Spanish lines.

(Below) *Fig. 47 Close up of the rosette made of tiny wooden pieces on the 'Tunbridge-ware' mosaic principle.*

Soundboards, temptingly plain and usually at the front of the instrument, therefore facing the audience, have often in the past been inlaid almost to a point where no original ground was discernible. Some of the baroque guitars were encrusted with tortoiseshell, mother-of-pearl, ivory, precious woods and even metals and stones. Few contemporary luthiers would approve of this practice today, on the basis that the soundboard, usually of spruce, is best left alone to do its job of amplification by reacting sympathetically to the vibrating strings. Apart from perhaps the delicate reinforcement of the soundhole rosette on a guitar, or the purfling of the soundboard edges

on the violin family, it is rare to find more inlaying than this in modern instruments.

Fingerboards, peg-heads and attachments are another matter. A fingerboard, usually of plain hardwood, may be enhanced with some advantage by the inlay of panels, either made up and inlaid as a unit, or applied one piece at a time. Peg-heads of lutes and the like are sometimes 'boxed' in a fine edge banding to emphasize the tapered delicacy of its form.

To summarize: grounds, if of solid wood or of wood veneer mounted on a composite board, may be almost any species, provided that they be seasoned and dry, therefore less prone to movement after inlaying.

Fig. 48 Ornate decoration is inset between plain sides to form this delicate purfling inlaid around the edge and down the centre of the back of the guitar. The purfling and the rosette were bought from a specialist supplier.

— 6 —

Sharpening

If I were asked to draw up a prioritized list of all the elements in the craft of woodwork to contribute by their perfection or obstruct by their faults, sharpening would appear at the top. No matter how skilled the craftsman, no matter how experienced in technical know-how, if the tools are defective, the work will always suffer.

We have all heard the saying 'A poor work-man blames his tools'. I disagree; blame the tools if they are incorrect, but exchange them or improve them, whichever is more appropriate. In the case of edge tools, improvement usually means that you must make them sharper.

Sharpening ought not to be regarded as a chore, but rather as the essential prerequi-site to the commencement of an important task, representing the craftsman's first step in the direction of quality work. My experi-ence as a tutor of craft topics is that students who least enjoy the sharpening process are those who have not learned the skills associ-ated with it. Obviously it is better to be shown the techniques by an experienced guide, rather than try to learn from a book or video, and that is what I recommend. Any qualified tutor of cabinetwork or joinery could teach the subject, since most of the tools involved will be common to all aspects of the craft. Such a person is worth seeking out and engaging to teach this aspect of the subject; until then, this guide should help.

As to equipment required to achieve the sharp edge on blades of every kind, there is a wide choice. I used to have an array of half a dozen 'stones', arranged in a pur-pose-made wooden case, ranging from very coarse carborundum grit through slate,

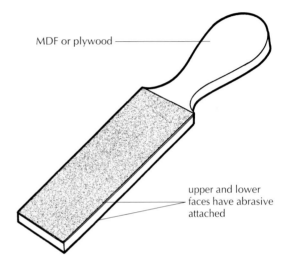

MDF or plywood

upper and lower faces have abrasive attached

Fig. 49 A useful hone made from sheet material, faced either side with suitable abrasives, usually of different grits.

Arkansas and leather. This used to be dis-played with some pride at demonstrations; now I have a combination of Japanese water stones, diamond hones and ceramic stones, varying in grit from about 1,000 to 8,000. Occasionally, I still strop a scalpel with leather if very fine work is needed, whilst at the coarse end of the kit I use a double-ended bench grinder to remove hefty waste when reshaping blades.

If operating on an austere budget, or if the fancy takes one to economize with a makeshift hone, it is acceptable to use an abrasive sheet fixed to a piece of flat mate-rial such as MDF; 6mm (¼in) thick should do. Several grades may be prepared from say, 240 to about 1,000 grit.

These shop-made hones may be shaped according to individual requirements and should not be regarded as inferior, since they perform very well and offer considerable savings. If they are relatively small they may be operated with one hand holding the blade and the other applying the hone. The blade may then be moved across the steady hone or vice-versa. From fine silica papers to very fine abrasives like Micromesh, the hones may be made to individual requirements.

Leather strops may sound old-fashioned, but charged with a compound such as jewellers' rouge it is possible to produce an unparalleled edge.

Bench stones need to be fixed in some way to prevent movement during the sharpening process. Some makes are supplied in a box with non-skid feet, such as the stones shown in the illustrations. A sturdy, stable surface is required to support the stone since the effort of abrading has the undesirable propensity to move the stone forward and back.

Here is an outline of techniques that will help you sharpen knife blades, purfling cutters and scrapers.

BLADE TYPE

Knife blades vary in design from thin to broad in section, from parallel to tapered, from pointed to blunt and from straight-edged to curved. I have a collector's attitude to tools, particularly to knives, with the result that I have more than I need, but it is no bad thing to have a choice, providing it doesn't get out of hand.

Any cutting edge is produced by reducing the blade's thickness by bevelling. This may be achieved with a bevel on one side, as is the marking knife or the draw-knife, for example. Our knives will require bevelling from each side and, whether thick or thin, a similar angle is applicable. I speak of the angle judged from either side of an imaginary centre line running through the length of the blade. If we aim to produce this bevel at about 5 degrees each side and if one is happier with the use of a physical guide, then it should be easy enough to make one by cutting out a 'V'-shaped gap of 10 degrees in a piece of card for reference. It is probably sufficient for most to draw a bevel angle with a protractor and use it as a visual guide with which

Fig. 50 The standard triangular blade that comes with some craft knives, honed to scalpel sharpness. The blade is fixed in a collet-grip handle allowing interchange of blades of different shapes and sizes.

to compare the appearance of the bevelled edge as it is being created. Alternatively, a 5 degree template may be made from card and used to refer occasionally to the angle at which the blade is held on the hone during the sharpening operation.

Inlaying needs only two types of knife: one that is thin-bladed, and a heavier, stiff-bladed knife.

THIN-BLADED CRAFT KNIFE, OR A STANDARD SCALPEL

Looking in more detail at craft knives of the variety found usually with disposable blades, it is better if the design incorporates a clamping device to ensure that the blade is fixed securely to the handle. Any tendency to move during the marking process may render the operation redundant from the start.

Implicit to the term 'disposable' is the suggestion that the blunted blade is redundant and should be discarded. However, it is possible to sharpen even the scalpel blade, virtually to its original pristine condition,

many times before replacement becomes necessary. This is helped by the fact that these types of blades are made from parallel section and may be rejuvenated almost to extinction. Tapered blades present a thicker section as the edge is sharpened, as will be shown below.

A HEAVIER-SECTION, STIFFER-BLADED KNIFE FOR INCISING AND CHOPPING

An extreme example of a thick section reduced to a fine cutting edge is an old-fashioned cut-throat razor. The reduction is in fact not a bevel but a concave radius to an unimaginably fine edge. Its brutal name, whilst pejorative, is nonetheless descriptive, but hopefully the inlayer will find more creative uses for it.

These blades may be bought in sophisticated barbershops, or, perhaps more appealing to our imaginative craftsman, they often turn up in second-hand shops at prices less than a tenth of the new price – even less, if the edge is badly serrated or the end broken off, rendering them useless for shaving.

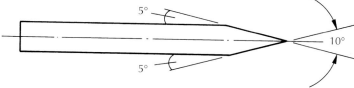

Fig. 51 A parallel blade with a double bevel, shown in section.

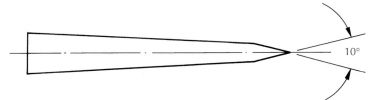

Fig. 52 The same double-bevel angle is used on a taper blade. Shown in section.

For our purpose these deficiencies do not matter as they will be ground away to create our custom shaped blade. Epoxy adhesive may be used to fix the blade shaft into a wooden handle, pre-drilled to accommodate it. There are endless possibilities, but this is not the place to detail them further.

Blades intended for chip carving and the like are suitable, providing they are not over-thick, since we have the need to cut into our ground with minimal width of cut. These may be tapered in section, that is, in effect, already partly bevelled from the back to the edge, requiring a secondary bevel to be applied to sharpen it. The same angular considerations are recommended as to the parallel blade detailed above.

TO SHARPEN KNIFE BLADES

Whether the blade is slender and parallel, or heavier and tapered in section, sharpening or honing is similar. Let us take for our example a bench stone, either water-stone, diamond or ceramic, since our primary consideration at the moment is geometry.

Laying the blade flat on the stone with the sharp edge pointing away, raise the back of the blade the required amount to incline the blade at the prescribed angle of approximately 5 degrees. Use whichever of the means is preferred to ascertain this as described above. Push the blade away, that is with pressure on the leading edge that is to be honed, trying to retain the angle and maintain a consistent area of contact with the stone. The latter point is important to create a bevel and not a convex face. Such a condition would be detrimental, since this would effectively increase the angle at the cutting edge.

On completion of the stroke, it is necessary to rotate the blade to bring the opposite face in contact with the stone. Raise the back edge, as was done in the first pass, to create the bevel and draw the blade along the stone with a pulling action.

It is important in rotating the blade that the blade is removed from contact with the stone, to avoid touching the sharp edge and risking damage to either blade or stone surface.

Frequent examination of the bevel is recommended, to ensure that the angular contact is being sustained. After a little careful practice, this comes with confidence and security.

When the edge is thought to be sharp, or close to it, there is the need for some judgement of what is meant by sharp. A practical way to approach this is to hold the blade under a bright light and look along the edge, rocking the blade from side to side to try to reflect the light on any flat spot or flaw. Objectively, one is looking for a 'candle', so-called; this is a bright reflection of the light source appearing as a spark or flash on the extreme edge of the blade. Ideally there will be no spark reflected, in which case there is a perfectly sharp edge, and this should be the aim. A disciplined approach to this examination is essential. Naturally for the incising of grounds for inlay work, the point requires especial attention.

SHARPENING BLADES FOR PURFLING CUTTERS

As has been mentioned earlier, the purfling cutter is used for marking or cutting channels for the inlay of purfling, rather than cutting the purfling itself, so should best be called a channel-cutter, but tradition has got there first. Whatever the name, its job is clear and that is to mark or incise with a small blade fitted to a device that incorporates a fence, or guide, permitting an incision to be made parallel with an edge, be it straight or curved. The

Fig. 53 A parallel-section blade at first stage of sharpening; back edge of blade (nearest the body) raised to bring the bevel flat on the stone and being pushed away.

Fig. 54 Return stroke; the blade is now being pulled towards the body with the opposite bevel in contact with the stone. As the bevel increases in width on either side of the blade, control is necessary to produce a balanced, symmetrical edge.

blades in question are provided with the cutter, unless of course the device is shop-made. In the latter case, or if the blade in the proprietary cutter is lost or worn out, replacement is a straightforward job. Most craftsmen will have access to broken hack-saw blades; if not from one's own work-shop, a polite request at almost any car repair shop should bear fruit. One hack-saw blade will provide enough blades to last a lifetime. A bench grinder is essential for this task to first form the end of the hacksaw blade to the required shape prior to parting it off. It is also best to hone the edge to sharpness before separating it from the main saw blade.

Shaping the blade for the purfling cutter is different from the knife blade, since it has a bevel on only one side of the blade but on both edges. This is to permit cutting in both directions along a periphery but leaving one side of the cut perfectly square to the face of the ground. This ensures a secure fit of the inlay, whereas, theoretically a bevelled edge will produce a slightly angled channel side. Please consult the diagrams to clarify.

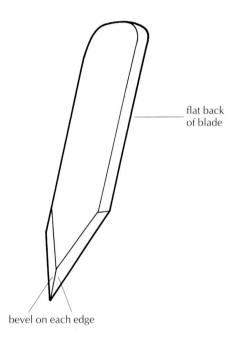

flat back
of blade

bevel on each edge

Fig. 55 For shallow incisions, this blade shape is ideal. There is a tendency for it to part the fibres in its path so, for anything deeper than say 1.5mm (⅟₁₆in), a chisel edge is better. The latter cuts a groove by removing rather than separating.

SHARPENING SCRAPER BLADES

At least two types of scraper are normal to our inlaying workshop, with variations in the type of blade and ways of sharpening, depending on the materials to be scraped and the results required.

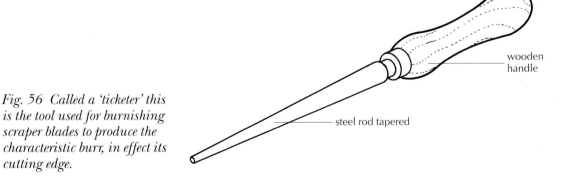

wooden
handle

steel rod tapered

Fig. 56 Called a 'ticketer' this is the tool used for burnishing scraper blades to produce the characteristic burr, in effect its cutting edge.

Taking the plain cabinet-scraper made from a rectangular piece of hardened spring steel, its cutting edges may be burred to enable a cutting action to be effected. The burr may be coarse or fine, though in relative terms it is the nature of the scraper to produce a light cut to enhance the finished surface without tearing the wood fibres.

Processing from scratch with a new blade we may consider the following sequence,

CABINET-SCRAPER

Remove any accidental burrs or other blemishes from the face of the scraper by rubbing it across the face of the stone

Flatten and level the edge square to the face. Setting the scraper at a diagonal during the traversing of the stone helps to keep the blade vertical thus making the edge square with the sides of the blade. A 'ticketer' or burnisher is used to produce the burr. This may be done by bearing down on the burnisher along the length of the blade.

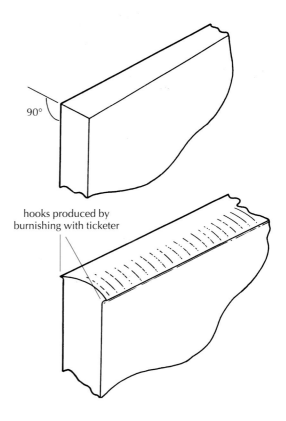

hooks produced by burnishing with ticketer

(Above) *Fig. 57 Top Square, clean edges essential features of the cabinet scraper prior to burnishing. Bottom: the blade after burring with the ticketer.*

Fig. 58 'Flatting' the blade edge to remove any old or redundant burr.

Fig. 59 Commencing the push stroke with the blade held vertically, its edge set at an angle across the hone. This helps to keep it upright as the hone is traversed.

Fig. 60 The stroke is completed with the same attitude of the blade to the hone.

(Above) *Fig. 61 Burnishing the scraper edge with a ticketer. Firm pressure is brought against the blade edge whilst stroking the ticketer up and down it.*

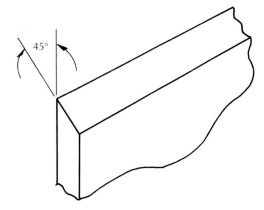

Fig. 62 Top: a blade from a scraper plane, or two-handed scraper. Unlike the cabinet-scraper, its edge is somewhat chisel-like and ground at 45 degrees. Bottom: the sharp edge has been burred over with the ticketer.

The blade may be held in a vice for this purpose, or simply rested on the bench top.

SCRAPER PLANE BLADE

Remove the burrs as per the preparation of the cabinet-scraper.

Grind or file the edge at 45 degrees to the face, then refine the ground edge on the stone. Lay the scraper flat on the bench with its bevel up and 'draw' the edge with the ticketer. Turn over the blade with bevel down and proceed to stroke the edge.

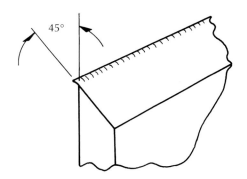

Fig. 63 Here the blade is bevelled as for the scraper plane. It is laid bevel down as the ticketer is drawn across the flat side to 'draw' the edge. This is the commencement of the stroke.

Fig. 64 Completion of the drawing stroke across the scraper; flat side, bevel down.

Fig. 65 Burnishing the scraper plane blade; the first stage is rubbing back and forth across the blade resting fully on the bevel.

(Below) *Fig. 66 Here the ticketer is shown having completed the first stroke.*

First, with the ticketer rubbing along on the bevel at 45 degrees to the face of the blade. This action is continued, gradually bringing the ticketer down until it is at 90 degrees to the face. This will produce a coarse burr that may be adjusted, by experiment, to give the desired cut. Remember that the idea is to get a fine shaving from the surface of the work, rather than a fibrous dust. A hand-held cabinet-scraper may be prepared in this way if a coarse cut is needed.

(Above) *Fig. 67 Having burnished the edge a score of times or more, gradually the ticketer is brought down until it is at right-angles to the table top, producing a burr in the process.*

Fig. 68 Scraping with the sharpened blade; bow the blade by pressing with the thumbs as the fingers restrain the sides. This stresses the blade reducing its flexibility and allowing the function of scraping to be performed.

— 7 —

The Holtey
Cutting Gauge

Carl Holtey is one of Britain's most highly respected experts in the world of high class woodworking tools. His prized examples of planes are mentioned in the section on tools beginning on page 13.

During one of many conversations between Carl and myself, the subject of specialized tools came up with regard to a tool for the cutting of channels for the embedding of purfling or corner banding. Specifying the needs in terms of the cutter, its action, the controls of depth and width, etc., I left the design to Carl, who produced the fine tool detailed here.

The handle may be rotated and locked in any position up to 90 degrees either way relative to the centre line of the main shaft. This feature permits the handle to be placed at whatever angle feels most convenient to the user. The cross-bar carries a knurled screw to tighten on the blade, allowing for adjustment of depth of cut.

Incorporated in the main shank is a screw with a knurled head that tightens on the cross-bar, permitting the setting of the distance of the cutter from the main shank. The latter serves as the fence, or guide as may be seen in Fig. 75.

No spanners or keys are needed to set up the cutting gauge, in fact as may be seen from Fig. 71, all its parts may be disassembled by hand.

Single blades to mark and incise channels or cut strips may be used in the gauge, or double blades, having been separated with spacing shims, used for cutting bandings or purfling if desired.

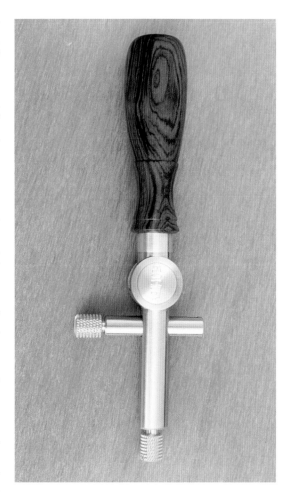

Fig. 69 Elegance and ergonomics are desirable features found all too rarely in modern tools. Here is an exceptional example of excellence in both respects.

The Holtey cutting gauge is shown in use in the next chapter.

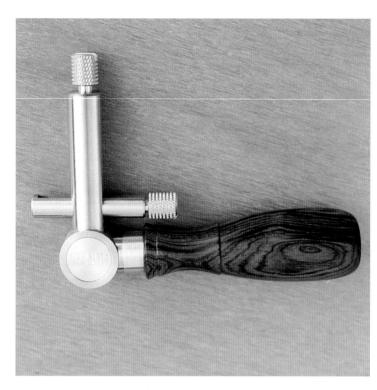

Fig. 70 By rotating the handle anticlockwise, its grip is released permitting it to be swung to any position up to 90 degrees either side of the main shaft.

Fig. 71 The Holtey cutting gauge in parts; it is easily dismantled for cleaning.

— **8** —

Inlaying Corner Banding
(First Method)

From Chapter 5 the reader may deduce that banding, being composed of one or more straight strips of veneer, may be taken to represent the terms of reference; binding, lines, purfling, stringing, etc. This is setting aside, for the moment, the purflings with 'sandwiched' cross-banded decoration within the strings.

For this method the Holtey cutting gauge is used. It is wise to carry out a test on a scrap sample before applying the cutter to the ground chosen for the inlay project.

The preliminary requirement is to set the depth of the cutter. As it is a square

banding the cutting gauge may be applied to both the face and edge of the ground to produce the desired recess. The same applies to the setting of the width. Aim to make the depth of cut slightly more than the depth of the banding, say about 5 per cent deeper than the banding depth to ensure that the waste comes away cleanly without leaving crumbs in the corner: cleanliness bestows its own rewards.

Prepare the edges to receive the corner banding by planing level, smooth and to whatever will be the finished size of the ground.

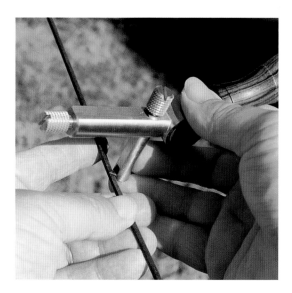

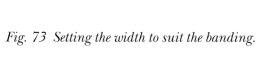

(Above) *Fig. 72 A single cutter blade is fitted and set to the depth of the banding.*

Fig. 73 Setting the width to suit the banding.

(Above) *Fig. 74 Preparing the edges of the workpiece by planing.*

Fig. 75 The cutting gauge is leaning forward to reduce the blade penetration for the initial cut. A more upright angle will be applied gradually until it is vertical, achieving the full depth of incision.

Holding the ground in a vice or some other clamp, the cutting gauge may be applied first along the face and then the edge, *across the end grain.* First cuts should be very light with the intention of merely marking the line. In the example shown the grain happens to run with the width, not the length, of the workpiece. The reason for this sequence is that with the likelihood of the cross-grain breaking out at the ends, such faults will be removed during the cutting of the long grain sides. The cutting action may be used in both directions if the blade has been prepared correctly (*see* Chapter 6).

Fig. 76 A waste piece has
been cut away from the
ground; it is almost identical
in section to the ebony banding
lying at its side.

Depth of cut is controlled by leaning the handle forward such that only a small amount of the blade is in contact with the surface of the ground, even though the blade is set at full depth. Bringing the handle to the vertical in steps as each subsequent pass is made takes advantage of the facility to graduate the rate of incision, thus reducing risk of breakout.

When full depth is reached, the cutting gauge is applied to the edge in the same manner as that described above resulting, hopefully, in a clean recess for the application of the corner banding.

Fig. 77 The sides are recessed
awaiting the fitting of the
banding.

Fig. 78 The two banded sides are glued and taped.

A trial fit should be carried out to ascertain correct size of recess has been produced and the remaining corners recessed. Reminder: it is advised that for four-sided grounds in solid wood, the best sequence is to recess the cross-grain sides first followed by the long grain.

The banding may be cut to length and mitred carefully with a dry run, without glue, in order to perfect the fitting. After a satisfactory dry fit, the banding may be glued in with any normal woodworking adhesive and retained under pressure using masking tape until dry.

If the depth setting was correct, there should be just a little of the banding to clean up with a scraper to level it with the ground.

Fig. 79 The finished inlay scraped clean and level.

Inlaying Corner Banding
(Second Method)

This method uses a combination of two proprietary tools: a Dremel Multi Model 395 tool fitted with a binding router attachment from Stewart MacDonald.

Very few people with an interest in lightweight woodwork or model crafting need an introduction to Dremel tools. The Multi Model 395 is their latest high-speed rotary power tool capable of performing many tasks when combined with its accessories, or those from other manufacturers. Important features of the 395 include a quick-change chuck and variable control of speeds from 10,000 to 37,000 r.p.m. It is used for this operation in combination with a binding router attachment, one of the new accessories available from the Stewart MacDonald Guitar Shop Supply.

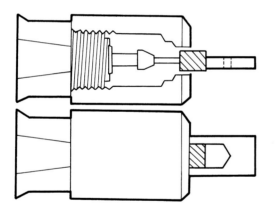

(Left) *Fig. 80 The upper view shows a cutaway of the side of the MacDonald binding router attachment. The cutter is wider than the bearing, so cuts away waste precisely to the extent of its projection. The lower view shows the cutter enclosed by the bearing giving support and security as it is rested on the surface of the workpiece.*

Fig. 81 Dremel's Multi Model 395 fitted with the MacDonald binding router attachment.

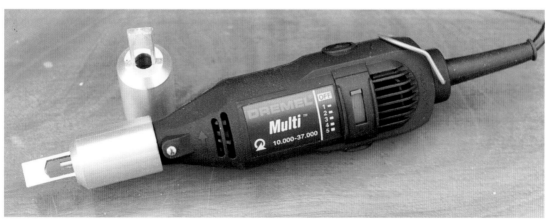

Fig. 82 Shavings stream away from the cutter in the routing tool.

Fig. 83 Marking the banding length prior to cutting with a mitre guide.

Fig. 84 Care is necessary when establishing the length of the fourth piece of banding, as it must fit the recess and at both ends.

Developed especially for recessing channels around guitar edges, it is excellent for cutting corner channels in other similar objects, with either straight or curved sides. Routing of channels from 1mm (½5in) to 3mm (⅗5in) with two different sized guides is a straightforward affair, with accuracy assured once set up correctly. As always, some trials are recommended on scrap samples before launching into the *magnum opus*.

For this project a piece of very ordinary pine was used, – not the easiest to wood inlay, since the alternating soft and hard grain tends to cause inconsistency in the progress of the cutter, often accompanied by tearing out of the soft grain. Nevertheless, using a tungsten carbide cutter in the router guide with the Dremel powering at about 30,000 r.p.m., the recesses were cut precisely, quickly and cleanly.

Operation of the Dremel/MacDonald combination is an almost foolproof way of producing a precise uniform recess. Laying the flat side of the guide on the face of the ground and maintaining contact with the back edge of the guide to act as a fence, the tool is steered along, happily removing waste in a very controlled manner.

It may be worth pointing out that it is best to follow the general rule of cutting cross-grain before the long grain, in case of breakout of the cross-grain at the ends. If this happens then the cutting of the long grain sides will clean up the broken ends. Alternatively, scrap blocks may be fitted temporarily as shields during the cutting operation, leaving clean corners on the workpiece.

Fig. 85 All four sides are fitted, glued and smoothed creating a framed tablet.

No break-out occurred in the machining of the given example and the recesses were clean and square with no need of further attention prior to embedding the banding.

Ebony banding was fitted into the recess with mitres cut carefully, to produce an attractive decoration on an otherwise commonplace material.

—10—

Inlaying Corner Banding (Third Method) and Stringing (First Method)

From the sophisticated we go to the simple, to demonstrate how with a little imagination the tooling may be shop-made, but this need not be inferior, rather it should be regarded as a custom-built 'special', economic and above all, effective.

A corner banding plus an inlaid string are to be embedded, separated by a space left in the ground to produce a wider decorative effect. Recessing for both the corner banding and the stringing is by the same tool, the shop-made scratch-stock.

Fig. 86   The workpiece is fixed securely and the scratch-stock applied by leaning it at a slight angle as it is pushed along with the blade in direct contact with the surface. Guidance of the cutter is obtained by keeping the scratch-stock fence pressed against the side of the workpiece during the operation.

Scratch-stocks are useful in producing a channel to a given size and depth simultaneously. The major difference between the purfling cutters described in earlier chapters and the scratch-stock is that the blade in the latter is presented to the ground sideways on, similar to a scraping action, as it were. Applying the blade in the same manner as a scraper requires it to have a square, sharp edge on each of the sides that will come into contact with the recessed channel. This is established at the grinding stage, and regulated by honing.

Making the scratch-stock is simply a matter of selecting a suitable piece of hardwood and cutting it to the details shown in the

Fig. 87 A clean rebated corner is produced by the scratch-stock. The latter is shown with its blade removed.

(Below) *Fig. 88 Simple scratch-stock. The two halves hold the blade at the required position to produce the correct depth of incision at the correct distance from the edge of the ground. Two holes are drilled to provide alternative positions for the wingnut and bolt, to permit a range of blade locations.*

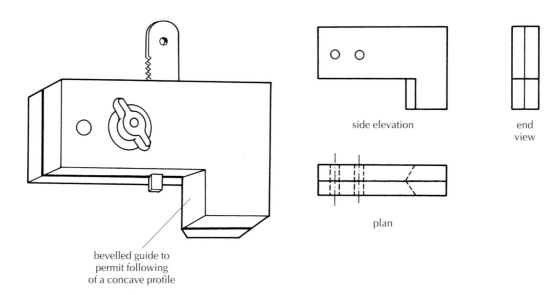

side elevation

end view

plan

bevelled guide to permit following of a concave profile

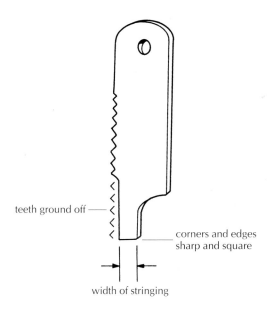

teeth ground off

corners and edges
sharp and square

width of stringing

Fig. 89 Scratch-stock blade made from a broken hacksaw blade. Care must be taken to grind the profile whilst keeping its face square to the edge.

drawing. It is best to make the blade-holder in one piece then saw it down the middle to produce the two halves.

Blades are made from scrap hacksaw blades ground to required sizes; it is best to create a new blade for each string as needed, creating different sizes that will remain in readiness for further use.

Retention of the blade at the correct distance from the fence, or the guide, if you prefer, is achieved by tightening the wing-nut on the screw that passes through the two sides of the stock. Two holes are drilled for alternative screw positions to accommodate different width settings of the blades.

Bevelling of the fence permits traversing of a concave profile such as a guitar side. It is worth pointing out the importance of producing a close fit between the sides of the stock and the blade, since if a gap exists, there is the risk of wood fibres clogging the joint and building up between the fence and the side of the ground. Frequent checks

are advised during the scraping process to see that no build-up is occurring.

Recess depth is increased progressively and gradually as with all such operations, keeping an eye on uniformity. Since many strings are barely thicker than a postcard, very few passes of the scratch-stock are necessary to achieve sufficient depth. Some may prefer to use a purfling cutter such as the special Holtey tool to mark and delineate the channel sides prior to scratching out the recess. This is no bad principle if working in a soft ground or one with a wild grain.

In application the scratch-stock is gripped in both hands for maximum control to maintain pressure of the fence against the side of the ground as the ground is traversed in the scraping action. As the stock is pushed forward it is tilted away for two reasons: to effect the scraping action, and to reduce the depth of early passes. The tool may be used in reverse by pulling, but to function correctly, the tilt must then also be brought towards the operator. A push-pull technique is ideal and not difficult to assimilate. Gradually the stock is brought more upright until it is vertical for the finishing passes, by which time the full depth of channel should have been reached.

In the given example, the corner banding is fitted first. The scratch stock is used to cut the recess for this, with the same blade as will be used to produce the channel recess. Of course, the blade is set close up to the fence for this first part of the operation, in fact, with a small part of the blade held within the fence. It is best to fit the corner banding before continuing with the cutting of the recess for the string, since this will protect the edge and give a secure bearing for the fence. Gluing and fixing with masking tape prior to cleaning up with a scraper is the next stage.

Proceeding with the embedding of the stringing is an almost identical operation to that of inlaying the corner banding. Of course, the blade width needs to be checked on a piece of scrap together with care in setting the required distance from the fence. In this example a strip of the ground is left as a spacer between the corner banding and the string.

Determining the width to suit the stringing is merely a question of experiment to determine a fit between the string and the recess. When the adhesive is applied, it may well have the effect of swelling the fibres of the inlay. Thus if there is much of a delay before fitting, there may well be a problem due to the expansion of the string spoiling what was a close but easy fit in the test stage. Of course, any liquid adhesive will expand wood fibres potentially, and that may work in favour of the inlaying process in principle, providing that the time in embedding after adding the glue is kept at a minimum.

When applying the glue, it is as well to consider that in the case of a string or other embedded inlay which is enclosed within a channel, there is the tendency for the glue to act as an air seal and hinder the embedding. Generally this need not be a problem if the glue is spread along the floor of the channel and not the sides. The embedding of the inlay will then force the glue up the sides without hitting a cushion of air.

As previously advised, the string and the surface of the ground may be levelled with a scraper and cleaned up ready for varnishing. More about the subject of varnishing is detailed in Chapter 21.

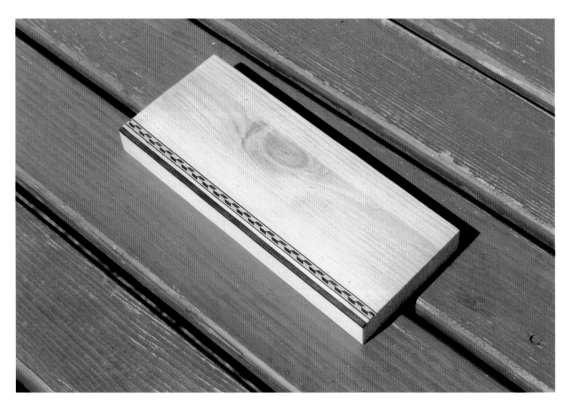

Fig. 90 An additional string was added in the softwood block after the corner banding was glued. It was produced with the scratch-stock in the same manner as for the corner banding recess. The cutter was ground to match the width of the string.

—11—

Inlaying Stringing (Second Method)

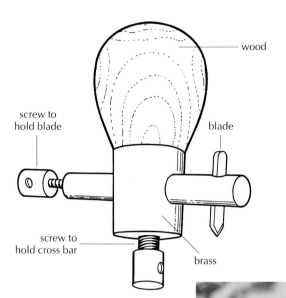

wood

screw to
hold blade

blade

screw to
hold cross bar

brass

String inlay is often associated with furniture, particularly where large areas of plain surfaces need a visual lift, such as table tops. In the following example, two tools are used to produce the recess; a small purfling cutter to delineate the channel and a hand router to excavate the waste.

A piece of rosewood was selected for this example, to represent a traditional item of furniture. The stringing inlay is also traditional in design, that of herringbone pattern enclosed with black lines.

To mark, cut and incise the channel the purfling cutter was used with a blade ground as detailed in Fig. 91.

(Above) *Fig. 91 Brass is used for the metal parts of this simple purfling cutter. The blade may be held at the desired depth by the end screw in the cross-bar. Its distance out from the central bar, or fence, is clamped by the lower screw.*

Fig. 92 A simple but effective purfling cutter set up ready to cut a recess for stringing in a piece of Brazilian rosewood.

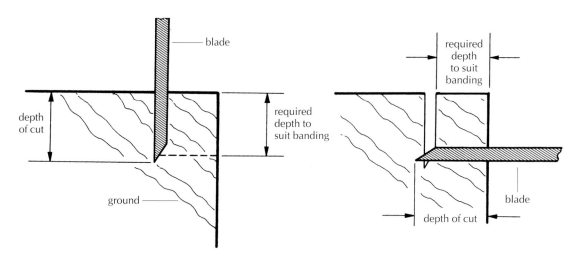

Fig. 93 A diagrammatic detail of the cutting of a corner channel. In the first cut, to establish the width of the cut, the depth is set to a little more than the depth of the banding. In the second cut the same principle is applied; the depth is set correctly, but the incision is slightly deeper to ensure a clean corner rebate.

Fig. 94 It was easier to set the ground in a vice and run the cutter blade along on the horizontal whilst controlling the cross bar with one hand and the handle with the other.

The preparatory step of running a test on a scrap sample was carried out before commencing work on the rosewood, as has been mentioned elsewhere in this book. No problems were encountered with this part of the operation. As may be seen in Fig. 94, the blade is applied in the horizontal with the working surface set in the vertical. This works very satisfactorily, as long as the depth of cut is controlled sensitively by the blade angle and the pressure of the right hand.

Excavation of the waste was then carried out with the hand router, removing a sliver of material to define the channel, then a secondary cut removed the remaining waste with one unbroken shaving. The workpiece was fixed between two bench dogs during the waste removal and the router controlled with both hands steering.

Fig. 95 Following the cutting of the channel sides, the recess was excavated with the hand router. Its efficiency may be judged by the single unbroken shaving of wood lying at the side of the workpiece.

Fig. 96 Clean joints and contrasting materials give a bright and effective delineation of the edge.

No cleaning up was necessary, apart from a brushing out of the channel as a precaution prior to gluing in the string. Care was taken in the setting of the depth, leaving virtually nothing to remove in the surface levelling operation.

Occasionally, when using strings made up of tiny decorative elements, as in the example given, pieces of the inlay may become detached. This is most likely to occur during the levelling or cleaning up operation, perhaps whilst scraping, assuming this is necessary. It is not too serious a problem, providing the detached piece, or pieces, is discovered and not swept up with the waste shavings. Prudent observation of the surface is essential after each cleaning stroke, whether using scraper, chisel or some other blade, or even abrasive paper. Any small part if retrieved may be returned to its rightful cavity, inserted and retained with a spot of glue, with little evidence of the repair.

12

Inlaying Stringing
(Third Method)

This is another method of channelling using the lightweight machinery from Dremel with the MacDonald purfling jig.

One of the advantages of the Dremel Multi Tool is that driving rotary cutters at speeds in excess of 30,000 r.p.m., a clean incision is forthcoming even with softwoods. I deliberately chose a piece of elderly pine with very wide soft grain to exemplify this capacity. Into this ordinary material I inlaid a piece of delectable stringing of cross-banded tulipwood enclosed in alternate lines of ebony and boxwood. And why not?

Developed for the routing of purfling channels in violin soundboards, or for soundhole inlays in guitars, or for any other operations where channels are required close to an edge, the MacDonald purfling jig is superb. A cutter of suitable diameter to match the stringing was mounted in the chuck and set to protrude the correct distance to suit the depth of channel. The distance of the cutter from the edge of the workpiece was adjusted by sliding the tool-carrier to the desired position and locking it with the thumb-screw.

To operate the jig it is best to clamp the workpiece down on to the bench top with space around it to swing the jig. It is

Fig. 97 Ready for channelling with the Dremel Multi Tool, fitted with the MacDonald purfling jig, loaded with a straight-sided router cutter.

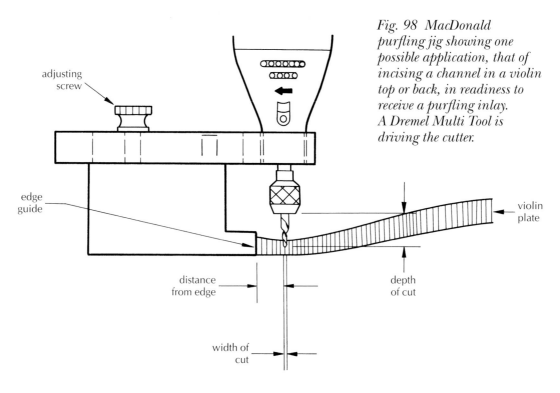

Fig. 98 MacDonald purfling jig showing one possible application, that of incising a channel in a violin top or back, in readiness to receive a purfling inlay. A Dremel Multi Tool is driving the cutter.

adjusting screw

edge guide

violin plate

distance from edge

depth of cut

width of cut

Fig. 99 A packing piece is placed between the clamp and the workpiece to permit access of the cutter. Hands are removed and the process has been halted for photographic purposes.

another example, shown clearly in Fig. 99, of the flexibility of the Wonder dog system of bench-top clamping. The base of the jig is then placed flat on the bench and the cutter brought to bear as the jig is traversed along the part to be recessed.

It was decided to cut across, as well as with, the grain to produce a corner stringing decoration as in a lid or box-top. With the speed set at about 30,000 r.p.m. the cutter removed waste cleanly without burning or tearing. Only a slight ragged burr was adhering to the top of the edge, as may be seen in Fig. 100, but this was removed without fuss presenting no impedance to the insertion of the decoration.

(Left) *Fig. 100 Since the cutter is rotating, it follows that the outer edges of the corners of the channel will be radiused. These will be squared later. Ragged edges left from the cutter on the surface will come clean after levelling.*

Fig. 101 The corner created by the intersection of the two channels was left with a radius from the rotary cutter and this was trimmed out square by a stabbing cut with a sharp knife.

Fig. 102 Before proceeding with the embedding, the channel was brushed out to ensure no crumbs were left from the routing to impede the operation.

(Below) *Fig. 103 In order to ensure clean corner joints of the stringing, a mitre guide was used to cut the lengths.*

(Bottom) *Fig. 104 Even common softwood may be enhanced with a decorative string.*

A mitre guide and knife were used to cut the tulip-wood stringing to length at 45 degrees. Razor-sharp knives are necessary, as always, for this type of cutting. Glue was brushed along the bottom of the channel and the stringing was retained with masking tape until the glue was set. Levelling was carried out with no misadventures.

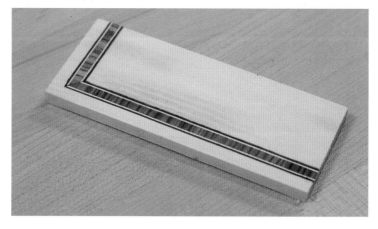

13

Inlaying Curved Stringing

Fig. 105 *With two blades, separated by a spacer, the Holtey cutter is being used to trace the sides of the string channel.*

Any of the methods detailed in the preceding chapters could be used to perform this particular operation, but for the sake of variety a different technique was used.

The objective was to apply a string line parallel to a curved edge; it might have been a violin soundboard, a shaped lid, or a serpentine top on a dressing table. I chose to use the Holtey cutter with two blades fitted separated by a spacer to give a double cut of the same width as the string line.

Common pine was used for the example with an ebony string line for the inlay.

Having clamped the workpiece to a bench top the Holtey cutter was drawn around the curve, maintaining secure contact of the guide against the edge. As always, the lightest incision was made at the commencement, followed by gradually increased downward pressure, combined with inclination of the blades, to delineate the channel.

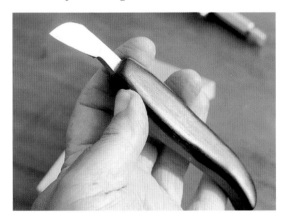

Fig. 106 *A fine-bladed knife used to increase the depth of the channel sides.*

Fig. 107 *Following the incised edges of the channel with the knife.*

Fig. 108 More downward pressure applied gradually to increase the depth of the channel sides.

(Below) *Fig. 109 A classic use of the toothpick chisel, seen here lifting the waste from the channel in one unbroken shaving.*

ing the waste in one continuous shaving.

Although it would have been possible to embed the string line directly in the channel without prebending, I chose to shape it first to eliminate any risk of breakage during the insertion. The inlay was actually flexible enough to have bent without heat, but a larger section would have been less obliging and might easily have broken without gentle heat to persuade it into shape.

To ensure the channel sides were deep enough, a secondary method was applied, on a 'belt and braces' principle. This was by incising with a very fine-bladed knife following the tracks marked by the cutter.

As may be seen by the illustrations, the incising of the channel sides was repetitive and gradual. Great care was taken to reduce the risk of slipping the blade out of the incision. It was then a simple matter to run the toothpick chisel along the channel, remov-

For this operation an electric bending iron was used, a specialist tool made for luthiers, but almost any heat source would suffice for such small sections. It should not be necessary to wet the string; dry heat as from a hot-plate or electric fire is fine, provided the usual safety precautions are observed. Whilst the string is hot and flexible, it may be fixed temporarily to the side of the curved workpiece and allowed to cool and take on a set.

(Top) *Fig. 110 Ready for insertion of the inlay.*

(Above) *Fig. 111 An electric bending iron used for curving the inlay.*

Fig. 112 After bending with heat, the string has been set to match the channel with little or no stress.

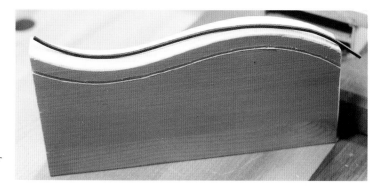

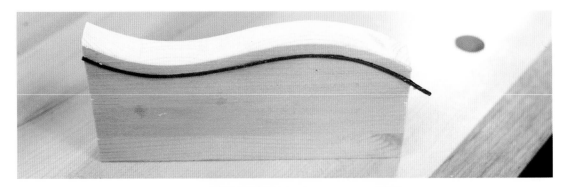

(Above) *Fig. 113 The string is embedded, requiring trimming to length.*

Fig. 114 Levelling with a cabinet scraper after the glue has set.

After a few minutes the tape can be removed and the string should be cool and fixed in its curve, ready for insertion. After gluing, the ends were trimmed and the surface scraped to leave the ebony line sharp and crisp-looking.

Fig. 115 The finished curved string inlay.

— 14 —

Principles of Excavation for Inlaid Motifs

Excavating recesses for banding, strings and lines is different from the methods used for inlaying motifs, panels, tablets and the like.

Using the term 'excavate' rather than 'create', in respect of the recessing of the ground to receive the inlay, satisfies terminological exactitude. Even so, some may relate excavation to the more crude 'digging out' of a hole in the earth. There is nothing crude about excavating a recess for the inlayer, since it must be made precisely to the measurements of the inlaid item, plus an almost unmeasurable margin to allow its admission. With regard to the depth of the inlay, theoretically speaking, the element to be embedded should be inset at as shallow a depth as possible, for the sake of speed and efficiency, among other considerations. It being borne in mind that, after embedding, the cleaning back of the related surfaces is likely to remove some ground and inlay simultaneously, due allowance for this operation must be made at the time of the preparation of the inlay and the calculation of its embedded depth.

INLAYING A RECTANGULAR PANEL

For the sake of a threshold example, let us take a rectangular panel as a typical subject. It follows that since the panel has three dimensions, so must the recess. Assume that the subject will be about as big as a postage stamp and of solid hardwood, about 1mm (1/32in) thick.

Clearly, the only facet of the panel that will be visible following the successful completion of the operation is its top. A close fit between the sides and ends and the excavated recess is of paramount importance. The thought that glue and varnish will make up any dissimilarities between the panel and the recess should be abandoned immediately as being detrimental to the aspirations of a craftsman and to the development of sound technical discipline. Recovering potentially spoiled work due to some unforeseen difficulty or an accident is another matter, and will be referred to later. To measure, mark and cut with optimum precision should become the normal intention of any craftsman, and of the inlayer in particular.

Our objective is to produce a 'negative' replica of the panel, as it were, in the ground. The latter is assumed to be a solid board of hardwood. First, we place the panel on the ground at the pre-determined location chosen for its final position. It is *possible* to measure the block and transfer the measurements to the ground, but this is not recommended, since fatal errors may occur in the process. Slight inaccuracies in measuring coupled with possible inexact transference of angles will lead to unacceptable gaps. It is probably unnecessary to remind the inlay student that discrepancies occurring in the cutting

Fig. 116 Outlining the panel with a pointed craft knife.

Fig. 117 A clearly defined edge, as yet with insufficient depth to proceed with excavation.

of the recess cannot be readily corrected, particularly if too much material has been removed from the length or width.

Having placed the panel in position, take the marking knife and mark the ground around the panel. An alternative to the knife is a collet-grip pencil used by architects and draughtsmen. These pencils are available with leads as fine as 0.03 mm supported by the finest of tubes, making a very controlled affair of marking. If the light source is adjusted to reflect off it, the line produced by the fine lead can be clearly seen. If practicable, it is best to clamp the panel in place to ensure its security during the marking operation. Acquiring the skill for the meticulous application of a knife blade is worth some detailed study, a prerequisite of which, however, is acquisition of the correct knife. It is recommended that if the reader has not

already done so, then they should refer to Chapter 2 before continuing.

Assuming a knife is used either for the marking or for the initial cut, it is best to mark from the corners towards the middle, to avoid an undesirable slip into the 'untouchable' area. This marking cut should not be very deep since its purpose is literally to outline the block. Mistakes may occur if this first cut is performed with more effort than is necessary, since the virgin ground is likely to resist indiscreet fumbling and turn the blade from its intended direction.

When cutting in the direction of the grain, the tendency will be felt for the blade to follow the soft grain between hard grain lines, as a train follows its rails. That is fine if the soft grain is straight and aligned with the required cut, but such good fortune is almost unheard of. Much

Fig. 118 'Ditching' the periphery of the excavation using a chisel.

more likely is that the grain *almost* follows the direction of the cut, with hard grain deviating and crossing the line, making a tricky job of steering the blade. All the more reason to underline the need for as sharp a blade as possible, coupled with the lightest application for the initial marking cut. Even after establishing the line, caution is recommended for several subsequent cuts as errors may still occur if one relaxes concentration.

Marking across the grain is easier to manage, provided, to repeat the rule, the light touch is maintained. The alternate soft and hard grain will be readily felt as the knife traverses, and if too hard a pressure is exerted the hard grain will be crushed and splayed leaving a crumbling edge that will spoil a clean marriage with the edge of the panel. Remember to continue to work from the corner to the centre of the lines.

Having secured the marking of its periphery, the panel may be removed and set aside. A soft pencil is used to mark the panel and the ground to ensure correct orientation for fitting later.

Deepening of the peripheral cut may now be undertaken by direct application of the blade inserted into the cut which is now used as a guide. The knife that was used for marking is probably adequate for this job. We are now concerned with producing the correct depth to suit the thickness of the panel. At this point, an indispensable device is the vernier calliper.

As the calliper is registered to measure the thickness of the panel, it automatically extends its depth-gauge by the same amount. This may be used effectively to set up the router and to help visualize the depth required for entry of the knife blade. It is easy to estimate the depth of the blade in the ground by observing the width at its point of entry. This becomes more reliable with practice and hopefully the student will acquire much of this skill prior to launching into the *magnum opus*.

Cutting continues to deepen the peripheral cut to a little more than the finished depth of the recess. This is to make sure that when 'bottoming out' the recess, there will be less likelihood of ragged corners or odd straggly fibres adhering untidily to the edges. Completion of the knife operation is by ascertaining that the corners are well defined by 'stab-cutting' them with the knife. This merely requires the placing of the point of the blade into the corner and pressing downwards to ensure that full depth is achieved. Stab-cut each side of each corner.

Excavation may now begin by applying a keenly sharpened bevel chisel to the task of 'ditching' the recess. This term refers to the process of making a small groove around the periphery of the recess to define its edge and depth prior to the levelling of the floor. It somewhat resembles the ditch around the sides of a field. Two chisels would be ideal, one to match the width and the other to match the length of the recess. If one's kit falls short of this unlikely state of perfection, use a chisel of less width. Trying to make do with one that is even the merest fraction bigger by skewing it at an angle is courting disaster, because the fine top edge of the excavation may be so easily destroyed by the shortcomings of inelegant manipulation of the chisel. A knife may be used to create the ditch by slicing along the edge on the waste side of course, but the knife lacks the required control in this application.

Note the recommendation to cut the ditches at the ends first, because the first ditching cuts are made in the direction of the grain. Try to judge the angle to remove material to the required depth of the recess. If unsure, then err on the shallow side, since rectification would be simply a matter of taking subsequent slices.

As the chisel is driven in, the student should beware of the lure to ease out the chip by prising before the cut is completed.

Fig. 119 Successful ditching delineates the periphery and prepares the recess for the floor-levelling process.

Fig. 120 A slightly bent fishtail chisel was used for deepening and levelling the floor of the recess.

Fig. 121 Completion of the excavation ready for the embedding of the panel.

If there is a feeling of stubbornness and the chip has not come away when the vertical peripheral cut is reached, then the probability is that insufficient depth was achieved by the knife. If a prising action is used in this situation there is every chance that a split will occur.

When the ditching is completed on all four sides, the levelling of the recess floor can be undertaken. The likelihood is that following the insertion of the panel the two components, insert and ground, will not be perfectly level. Rather than leave to chance this highly important feature, it is best to aim to leave the panel high, since it is obviously easier to level the panel to the ground, rather than the other way round. Setting down of the floor of the recess must therefore be of such depth as to leave the embedded panel high. As to the amount of protrusion of the panel, it needs only the merest fraction of a millimetre to be left for cleaning back.

So, to the levelling of the floor. Three methods are available. The most basic is to use the same chisel(s) used for the ditching, laid bevel-down to remove the waste. Chisels with slightly curved blades allow a more satisfactory ergonomic application and lend themselves to accessing the floor and corners of the recess more efficiently. This requires some skill in the manipulation of the chisel, since it is controlled by manual dexterity alone.

A visual guide is provided by the depth of the ditching, of course. Checking frequently for depth may be carried out with the depth gauge on the calliper.

A secondary method and, in my opinion, a superior one, is to use a hand-router for

Fig. 122 After gluing and taping the inlay in place, extra weight was added for security.

the floor levelling. This splendid tool, as was seen in previous examples, will level and set the correct depth simultaneously. Again, the use of the depth gauge on the vernier calliper may be used for setting the protrusion of the blade in the router. Blade protrusion may be extended progressively, working on the principle that 'a little, often' is generally better than one indiscreet hack.

A third method is to use a small motorized router of the Dremel variety, that may seem to the uninitiated a rather brutal piece of equipment. It is in fact not much different in size to the average electric shaver and capable of very refined work. Some of the best inlaying I have ever seen was produced with such a tool, by a chap who inlays mother-of-pearl decorations into fingerboards for musical instruments.

The use of the machine router is dealt with separately in Chapter 15.

EMBEDDING THE MOTIF

Our panel may now be inlaid, having been prepared for insertion before the excavation. It is best if just one gentle trial is attempted, without adhesive and without pressing fully home, to ascertain the accuracy of the fit, or lack of it.

As with other embedding, glue is spread lightly on the floor of the recess allowing the easy insertion of the panel without fear of an air lock or bubble. Excess glue will escape from the edges and ensure a secure fixing for the motif. Fix with tape and a clamp, suitably cushioned to avoid bruising and clean back the surfaces when dry.

Fig. 123 A scraper was used to level the surface after the glue had set. A rub with oil enhanced the grain of both ground and inlay.

TROUBLESHOOTING

If the required depth of the recess has been exceeded it is possible to add a sub-layer onto the bed of the recess beneath the panel, to raise it in compensation. An option is to fix with adhesive a layer of veneer to the underside of the panel, achieving the same result.

If the recess is too wide, by say, the thickness of a thumbnail or less, it may be possible to compress the panel on a vice or by hammering. Whilst caution must be present during this operation, to avoid over-stressing, the width may be increased appreciably. Not so the length; that will remain virtually unaltered.

Soaking the panel will also increase its width, but there is no guarantee that it will not shrink later. Another way of correcting excess width is by packing the sides of the recess with veneer, or alternatively, attaching veneer to the sides of the panel. The packing material may be taken from scrap retrieved from the ground. This is harder to achieve if the length of the recess is over-size because this calls for a cross-grain packing which is more difficult to cut and difficult to match. The best way is to cut a cross-grain piece of, say, twice the required size and trim back to size after attaching to the panel with adhesive.

None of the above methods is as good as starting from scratch with a fresh ground, but that may not always be possible.

When levelling the recess floor it may be necessary to use a router blade with a more pointed edge in order to clear the more intricate corners. If this presents a problem it is possible to tease out those less accessible portions with the toothpick chisel mentioned earlier.

—15—

Inlaying Motifs of Curved or Irregular Shapes

The previous chapter dealt with recessing to suit a rectangular motif. Other shapes, less formal without straight lines, such as oval or floral motifs, are dealt with similarly but need more care at the marking-out stage.

Caution when initiating the marking cut cannot be over-emphasized, since the curving lines are sometimes crossing grain at an angle and sometimes in the direction of the grain. It is the lack of consistency in the travel of the blade as it encounters different grain conditions that creates the problem of directional control. There will probably be advantage in changing the direction of travel of the blade from time to time, depending on this situation.

The aim is to inlay an oval motif of floral marquetry using the MacDonald router base attached to the Dremel Multi Tool. A piece of Brazilian rosewood is selected as the ground.

Marking may be done with a piercing tool made from a needle set in a wooden handle. Its sharp point should be held scrupulously close to the edge of the motif; the line it produces is fine but well-defined.

One may embed this type of motif with its protective backing paper uppermost and remove it in the levelling operation after fitting. Either way, the marking and excavation must be produced to receive it without reversing it, since the motif may not be symmetrical.

The routing base is fitted to the Dremel tool by screwing it onto the threaded nose. Depth setting is an accurately controlled

Fig. 124 Accurate depth of cut is achieved by the fine adjustment that is available with the MacDonald router base.

Fig. 125 Many cutters, bits and burrs are available to fit the Dremel tools.

(Below) *Fig. 126 · Tracing the edge of the motif with a needle point.*

affair with the adjustment facility incorporated in the design of the MacDonald tool. A fine cutter is best for this routing job, to enhance its precise nature. A very large choice of cutters is available but the ones described as 'downcut bits' are best for recessing and floor levelling, leaving a clean cut face.

Fig. 127 Following the line and clearing the edge of the recess.

(Below) *Fig. 128 Clean excavation is a feature of this tool; uniform depth is a by-product.*

Begin by lowering the rotating cutter bit close to and inside the marked line. The wide aperture in the base of the tool allows constant visual contact throughout the routing procedure. Initially the periphery of the motif is traced at the required depth leaving only the slightest amount of waste inside the line to clear on the second pass.

When cleaning up to the line it is best to try this as one continuous sweep, to avoid inconsistency on re-entry or re-starts. Not easy, but with a bit of practice on a scrap sample it is achievable. Having a ditch around the oval, it is a simple matter to remove the rest of the waste, but be methodical. Enlarge the ditch to leave clearance for the cutter before working from side to side, tracking with overlapping kerfing to leave the floor as flat as possible.

Scrape the recess floor to ensure flatness and uniform depth before gluing in the motif. Ensure security of the embedded motif by slight undercutting of the recess. Gluing and clamping with paper separating the clamp faces is recommended. Refer to the troubleshooting section in the previous chapter if snags are encountered.

When setting in and cleaning back, remember how thin the motif is and restrain the scraping, consistent with producing a fine level surface, of course. It is worth stressing once again the importance of aiming to leave the motif slightly proud of the surface of the ground.

Fig. 129 Clamp applied during gluing process. Paper is used to prevent excess glue adhering to clamping pad.

(Below) *Fig. 130 It is prudent to scrape with sensitivity to avoid tearing the motif.*

Fig. 131 The finished motif.

16

Inlaying a Motif and
Line Combination

In this chapter the project is to combine several motifs and associate them in an ensemble suitable for, say, a box lid or a decorative panel. Hand tools are used throughout to inlay the proprietary motifs and standard lines.

It is necessary to trim the corner motifs after removing them from the temporary grounds in which they are delivered from the manufacturer. This should be undertaken with great care since the outer portions of the design may become detached, if handled roughly. The lines that will be applied to join the two corners should be passed through the Wearing thicknessing tool to bring them to uniform size. Their delicate nature invites close scrutiny, after all. Thicknessing should be done before creating the scratch-stock blade to the required width, obviously.

In order to reduce the levelling process to a minimum, the ground should be prepared to size and given a flat and smooth, but not polished, surface.

Try to visualize the best positions in accordance with the proportions of the motifs and

Fig. 132 Two corner motifs. They come supplied in a protective ground from which they must be trimmed.

lay out the selected elements before marking. When a satisfactory arrangement has been established, mark the outlines of the corner motifs first. Do not assume that they are identical; they may not be, so, better to work on them individually and be sure to keep them separate.

Use either a scalpel blade, needle point or fine lead draughting pencil to mark the outlines of the motifs. No need to mark out the channels for the lines at the moment. Having marked each field in pencil with some identification to be sure of inlaying each motif in its own recess, set them aside for the moment.

Using a scalpel or craft knife, trace the pencil marks with the lightest touch, barely inserting the point of the blade. All that is required at this first pass is to emphasize the outline of the motif; this requires a disciplined concentration.

Cautious care then are the words to describe this marking procedure. Having completed the outlining with the knife one may continue to increase the depth of the cut a little at a time. Each subsequent pass should be little more than resting the knife firmly, rather than a heavy bearing, since the primary intention is to follow the line accurately. Only a few seconds are involved in the operation anyway, so no great saving is available by hurrying; better to take a few more light passes than risk straying from the incised path of righteousness.

Judge by the amount of inserted blade the depth reached by the point. For instance, in the case of the knife being used in the demonstration, it is triangular. Having

Fig. 133 Using a fine-pointed collet pencil to mark motif positions.

Fig. 134 A razor-sharp pointed blade for secondary marking and incising the periphery of the recess.

(Below) *Fig. 135 Excavating the recess with the hand-router.*

measured it I know that its insertion is twice the width at any given point, that is, if the exposed blade measures 1mm nearest the surface of the ground, the depth of cut is 2mm. Since most motifs are not much thicker than a hefty postcard, the necessary depth is not particularly difficult to achieve.

Carving out the waste in the excavating process is a different matter. The recommendation is routing by machine-router or hand-router; as may be seen in the example, the latter tool was used.

Make the edge on the router blade as sharp as possible and set its depth at half the thickness of the motif. If a vernier calliper is available it would be well-employed for this job.

It is best to work around the periphery removing a strip at a time, using short strokes into the incised outline. This is done with optimum control, pushing down and forward, constantly ready to pull back or stop the forward movement if there is the slightest danger of overshooting the line. When a shallow trench has been made all round, the central section may be removed to produce a provisional 'floor'.

In resetting the router blade for the final depth, recall that when levelling it is probably best to remove superfluous material from the motif than from the surface of the ground. Assess the depth needed to leave the very slightest amount of the motif protruding and set the blade accordingly. For example, measure the thickness of the motif and reduce the amount by, say, 5 per cent and set the blade to remove waste to that depth.

Care is still required even though the edges of the recess may be well-defined. Slips may still occur in the routing and it is all too easy to remove a piece of the periphery by accident.

Use the toothpick chisel to tease out the corners and ensure that no crumbs are left to hamper the embedding of the motif.

One 'dry' run, without glue, should suffice to check the fit of the motif in the recess. There should not be any discrepancies, but if there are it may be useful to look over the section on 'Troubleshooting' in the last chapter.

Assuming that all is well up to this point in the project, it is best to embed the motifs before continuing with the inlaying of the lines. A hammer was used to apply pressure to embed the motifs, and clamps were used with pads for absolute security. An example of this procedure is shown in the

Fig. 136 Teasing out the waste from corners inaccessible to the router blade.

Fig. 137 Not hammering, but pressing with the hammer head to localize pressure for the embedding process.

last chapter. It is wise to place a piece of paper between the clamping pad and the motif to obviate the possibility of a sticky problem if glue escapes.

In arranging the elements to be inlaid, consideration must be given to the placing of the lines, to verify not only that they will connect the two motifs satisfactorily but that they also lie parallel to the edge of the ground. The reason for the latter condition is to permit the use of a purfling cutter, using its fence as a guide along the edge of the ground.

A double blade arrangement installed in the Holtey cutter was used as detailed in Chapter 13. A single cutter could be used, setting up for two incisions laid side by side to achieve the same result, of course. In fact, since the lines are parallel and straight, the channel cutting could be achieved with a steel rule and a knife.

Before incising the channels for the lines, needless to say, a test run with scrap material was made. Following this, a careful pass was made along the ground without actually incising, to be sure that the distance from the edge was correctly positioned to connect the elements as planned.

The practice of lightly scoring with the blades, as a preliminary contact before the actual incising, should now be a habitual protocol, if the previous projects or the accompanying advice have been assimilated. In this particular case, since the grain ran with the length, in a strong fibrous material, all the more discretion was needed to guard against the cutters tracking a strong grain that deviated from the essential line. This condition is not dangerous if the grain runs in towards the centre of the ground, because the fence bearing against the edge prevents the blades from

Fig. 138 Using the scratch-stock for excavating the channel for the lines.

following. If, however, the grain wanders towards the outer edge, effort must be made to dissuade the blades from potential misdirection. Assuming the channel-cutting is achieved successfully it is then necessary to remove waste. A toothpick chisel could be used, but a more satisfactory effect is achievable with the scratch-stock on account of its ease of manipulation using its fence as a secure guide together with the facility to regulate the depth of the recess by setting the blade correctly. Care must be exercised in grinding the blade width to suit the line to be inlaid and – need I repeat it? – try it on a piece of scrap, first.

Removal of the waste should not present a problem if the foregoing suggestions are heeded, though it is worth mentioning that extra care should be taken at the ends of the channel, where contact will be made between the lines and the inlaid motifs. Leave nothing to chance in this respect, and use the toothpick chisel to remove the waste immediately in front of the embedded motifs prior to the application of the scratch-stock.

When the waste has been excavated to the correct depth and the toothpick chisel has been employed if and where necessary to remove any superfluity from the channel, it is brushed clean to accept the line.

A small amount of glue is laid into the channel and the lines applied with pressure and retained with masking tape until dry. Routine cleaning up of the surfaces of all the inlaid elements and the ground should not present any problems if the preceding stages have been carried out correctly. There is always the inherent possibility that a small piece of the inlay may pop out during the

(Above) *Fig. 139 All elements embedded satisfactorily, cleaned back and lightly oiled.*

levelling. If this does happen, it is most likely to be in the initial passes of the scraper. Therefore it is during the early part of this operation that scrupulous examination be given to the inlays, hopefully to discover nothing missing. If a portion has become detached, providing that it is recoverable, not damaged and is complete, it should be an easy matter to replace it with a dab of glue. Thorough drying should follow before a return to the scraping operation, hopefully to reveal an attractive inlaid decoration.

Fig. 140 Detail of fingerboard panel of a lute (see overleaf) made from rosewood with tulip-wood stringing. A fine ebony and pear purfling is added to decorate the pointed 'moustaches' where the fingerboard and soundboard meet.

Fig. 141 A Renaissance lute made by the author with inlaid panel in the fingerboard (see detail on previous page).

17

Inlaying a Rosette

There can be little doubt that the feature most likely to produce expressions of admiration from the beholders of a high-class guitar, is the rosette.

We presume that the instrument to receive the rosette is a fine example in the Spanish style, classical in design, and not a modern version with a plastic ring masquerading ineffectively as a traditional rosette. This decoration surrounds the so-called soundhole and imparts some additional rigidity and protection to that part of the soundboard. It might be claimed that the contemporary plastic ring is equally effective in mechanical terms, but the appearance of the traditional version is likely to gladden more hearts.

The construction of the rosette need not greatly concern the inlay student, since it is the type of motif that is bought from a specialist supplier. Rosettes are simple, sophisticated or astonishing in their complexity, varying in diameter to suit different instrumental needs. Generally they are about 1.5mm (⅟₁₆in) in thickness and made on the 'Tunbridge ware' principle.

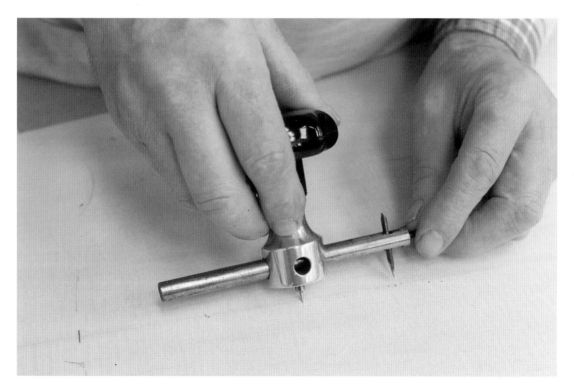

Fig. 142 Circle-cutter by an unknown German maker.

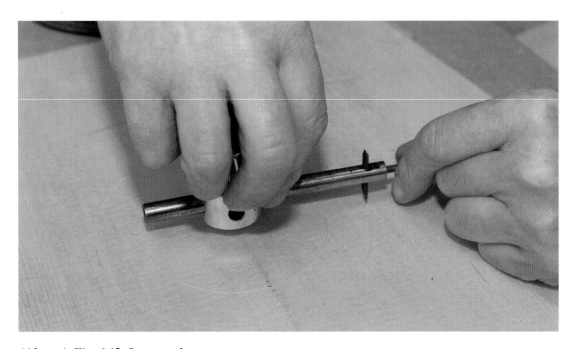

(Above) *Fig. 143 Inner and outer diameters are cut to depth with the circle-cutter, the blade of which is bevelled to cut in either direction.*

Fig. 144 The irregularity of the rosette is exaggerated to illustrate the principle of establishing the inner and outer diameters.

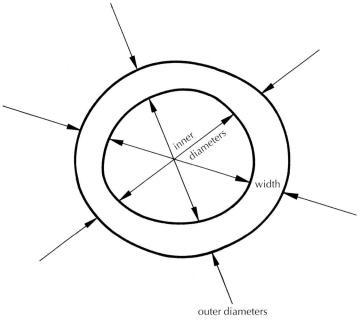

inner diameters

width

outer diameters

Some special considerations are necessary with regard to the dimensions of the rosette. Inner and outer diameters may vary slightly due to slight differences in the elements within the design. A high-class product will have less variation than an austerity model, but nevertheless, in principle, there is the need to proceed with caution.

In order to establish the diameter of the rosette, it is important to appreciate that a single measurement across the diameter is possibly insufficient, bearing in mind the potential for irregularity as mentioned above. Take the inner diameter first. Several measurements should be taken around the clock, so to speak, taking the average of these to assume the mean diameter. Measure the width of the rosette, also at several points around the ring to find the average. Multiply this by two and add the result to the mean inner diameter, the sum of which should produce the average outer diameter. Verify this by drawing with a compass the inner and outer diameters on a piece of card, and place the rosette in position with pins inserted around the periphery to hold it in place temporarily whilst inspection takes place. If the measurements were taken sensitively the rosette and the scribed circles should match. If not, it should be apparent where deficiencies lie and adjustments may be made accordingly. For sure, whilst a minimal amount of flexing may be exerted on the rosette to increase or decrease the diameters, it is not possible to change the width. That is why it is more accurate to add the width of the rosette rather than measure the outer diameter separately. A test to help prove this would be to draw around the rosette and then construct circles with a compass to match.

There are likely to be other methods but I have had no need to seek them since the way described above has worked perfectly many times.

Cutting the incisions for the rosette may be performed in several ways, too. A simple way would be to prepare card templates, produced as the foregoing test suggests. Provided the card is rigid enough, it will serve for making templates for marking the circles. The rosette itself is generally too flexible to be used as a template, but I have seen it done this way and inlaid successfully.

The most reliable and normal technique is by use of the circle-cutter as shown in the accompanying plates. Whatever the design of the circle-cutting tool, it is almost certainly going to have a point to determine the centre of the rosette and act as a pivot during the incising. It must also have a means of holding a blade securely, incorporating adjustment for depth and radius width. A few special accessories are available for attachment to routers, but my preference is for the type shown in the photographs, combined with the hand-router for excavation. The procedure is as follows.

Having determined the sizes of inner and outer diameters of the rosette and marked its intended position on the soundboard, or other ground, the blade is set in the circle-cutter to the radius of the inner circle. With the intention of embedding 95 per cent of the thickness of the rosette into the ground, measure that amount on the cutter blade to judge the depth of the incision. Remember to cut slightly deeper than the floor of the recess to ensure clean corners where the sides meet the floor. The operation of cutting the channel sides is uncomplicated, particularly since the lateral control comes from the centre pin leaving the hands to concentrate primarily on consistent depth of the incision. When the inner circle is incised, the same procedure is applied to the outer diameter.

Use of the hand-router is detailed in earlier chapters and leaves little to be added here, except to say, since the soundboard is made from straight-grained wood of a close texture, it will cut readily in any direction, but beware of becoming overconfident – an accident is always hovering, ready to strike the unwary. Set the blade of the router at about a quarter of the depth for the finished recess and proceed to work from the centre of the recess towards the incisions. As with other examples, if the edges are cleared first, it is easy and safer to

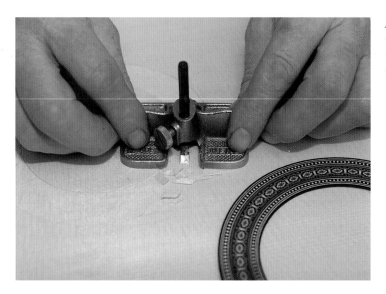

Fig. 145 Hand-routing is a very efficient and satisfying way to excavate and level the recess floor.

remove waste from the centre of the recess. Repeat this until the full depth is achieved.

Gluing in of the rosette should present no problem, following a dry run to see that the size of the recess matches. A block and clamp with the usual paper 'washer' between should be applied to be certain of bottoming the rosette to the floor of the recess.

After thorough drying, the inlay and ground should be levelled with a scraper, applied with care and frequent visual inspection to detect any detachment of parts of the inlaid element.

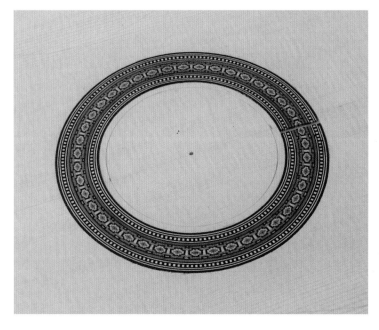

Fig. 146 The rosette is fitted and finished. An inner circle has been marked in readiness for cutting out the soundhole.

— 18 —

Inlaying Purfling

As mentioned earlier, musical instruments, mainly the stringed family, have for centuries provided craftsmen with vehicles for decoration, and most often with inlay – to the possible detriment to their acoustic qualities, some may say, but that would be difficult to prove, however logical.

In the violin family there is a case for inlay performing the dual function of ornament and support, as in the application of purfling around the edges of the top and bottom of the instrument. The inset purfling actually binds the grain, especially the soft spruce soundboard, helping prevent splitting of the vulnerable areas where end-grain is exposed. Little or no effect on the acoustic properties would occur as a result of this inlay, since it is placed over the ribs and does not encroach into the area of the instrument's vibrating plates. In any case, by now, all violins are purfled thus and if there were any detectable effect on the sound-producing properties, due to the inlay, it has become an accepted characteristic of the instrument. From the run-of-the-mill fiddle of basic student quality to the Cremonese masterpieces played by virtuosi, purfling has become a standard decoration common to all.

Amazingly, the same disarmingly simple type of inlay is used throughout: a string made up of three pieces side by side, in a black/white/black arrangement. The outer black lines are usually ebony and the nominally 'white' is generally sycamore, occasionally the more richly coloured pear. The width varies to suit the differing sizes of the instrument's family from violin to contra-bass, to satisfy the observation of proportional aesthetics demanded by the craftsman and the player. Despite the apparent similarity suggested by a casual glance, close examination of a fine master-crafted instrument, by an expert, will reveal subtle characteristics in the refinement of the application that will identify the maker.

In the viol family, the early cousins of the violin, purfling is not always restricted to the edge of the instrument but it may also be applied to the other flat areas such as the back. Geometric forms are extended from the edge purfling in designs with their origins in Celtic and Moorish knot patterns. Here the maker has some intellectual appraisal combined with artistic subjectivity to decide which elements in the design are to 'cross over' others. At points where the lines appear to cross, one over the other, the object is to emphasize the illusion by cutting the inlays to give an over-and-under effect as in weaving.

And here is how you do it.

Taking the back of a treble viol as an example; it will be already fixed to the ribs, those are the sides, of the instrument. In constructional terms, the body of the viol will be finished. Frequent movements of the workpiece will be necessary, so it is important to cover the work-top with a resilient non-skid cloth to prevent damage to the soft soundboard.

Work on the purfling begins with tracing the design with a well-sharpened pencil, or with one of the fine-leaded draughting types with the collet grip. A compass may be used as a guide to outline the edge inlay,

Fig. 147 Precise marking of the design is essential as the first step.

give the weaving effect. This first incision, as in all cases, should be light and faithful to the pencil line. I find it is a supplementary opportunity of refining the pencil mark by removing small deviations found in the original marking. For the following of the edge channel, it helps to guide the knife to use a spare finger, as if it were a fence, against the side of the viol.

Having defined the line with this incision, it is necessary to establish the second line and this requires some careful consideration. It should be remembered that it is normal practice to apply 'Scotch', or hot glue for fixing the purfling. (And all the other parts of the instrument; *see* Chapter 20.)

A word about channel width. Hot glue will swell the purfling, so allowance must be made in estimating its fit in the channel. In testing, as always, verify the size on a piece of scrap; try to achieve an easy, slide-in, match between the purfling and the channel, without pressure.

Take the odd-legs dividers, place the longer leg in the incised line and track around it, cutting the second line with the shorter leg, automatically parallel with the first. Some fastidious care must be taken with stops and starts of lines and especially where they cross over. These areas may need to be refined with the knife.

After completion of this initial definition of the channel, the incision must be deepened to accept 95 per cent of the depth of the purfling. Use the knife for this purpose, measuring with the vernier calliper along the blade to assess how much of the point to insert to achieve the correct depth. At this point it is worth reiterating the principle that this incision should be *slightly* deeper than the floor of the channel, to ensure clean corners where the sides meet the bottom. In this operation, work the knife from the corners with a slightly downwards stabbing action, drawing away along the lines, to be sure of producing clean channels at the ends.

or a Holtey-type guide with twin blades if available. Top and bottom extensions of the edge purfling is a more freehand affair, but with a rule to measure and assist with marking, it should not present a problem. Light marking with the pencil permits some correcting if accidents happen. Obviously, a pre-planned design should have been made for reference before starting to mark the instrument.

When the pencil line is completed it is necessary to incise it to the correct depth for the channel. Several ways are possible but I suggest the following. Incise one of the two lines all round the pattern, observing where the design stops and starts to

Fig. 148 'Odd-legs' in action marking the double recess for the purfling channel.

Fig. 149 Waste removal with the toothpick.

Fig. 150 Down-stabbing to produce a clean and vertical cut for precise mitre joints.

(Below) *Fig. 151 Marriage of the elements during the fitting calls for patience, discipline and aesthetic discernment.*

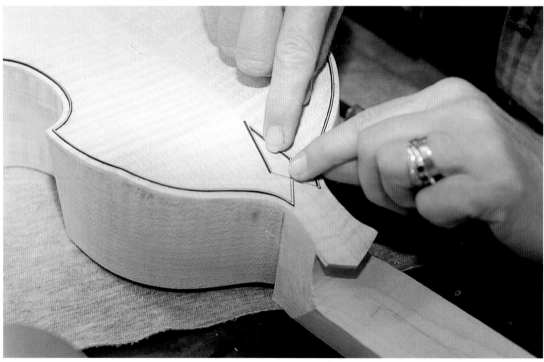

When this stage has been completed, it remains to excavate the channel by the removal of the waste. For this, the toothpick chisel comes into its own. There is a sense of satisfaction as the waste is eased out of the channel and the redundant material pops out. Best to work on short portions at a time, with frequent measurements being taken to verify the accuracy of the depth being reached. Use a small piece of the purfling to check, or set the depth gauge on the vernier calliper, for testing, if it is narrow enough to enter the channel.

If the waste is cleared all round and every superfluity removed (inspect with a lens to be absolutely sure of this), the next stage is the delicate fitting of the purfling.

Accurate preparation of the purfling is of paramount importance. The length and mitre angles are crucial, imposing the need for some trial and error. Remember, it is not possible to squeeze in an oversize length of purfling without it showing by some distortion somewhere. Neither is it possible to make up a gap, caused by a deficiency of length, with some type of paste filler; a disguise that will not only be easily detected, but which may even emphasize the fault.

Cutting the purfling to length is best carried out with a chisel used in a downwards shearing action. This makes it easier to produce not only a vertical face but also a straight line cut for a precise mitre joint.

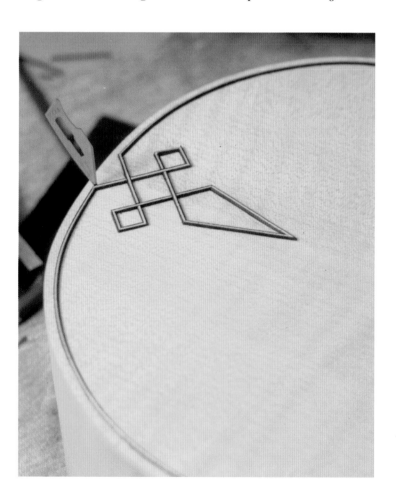

Fig. 152 At this stage the purfling is proud of the face of the ground.

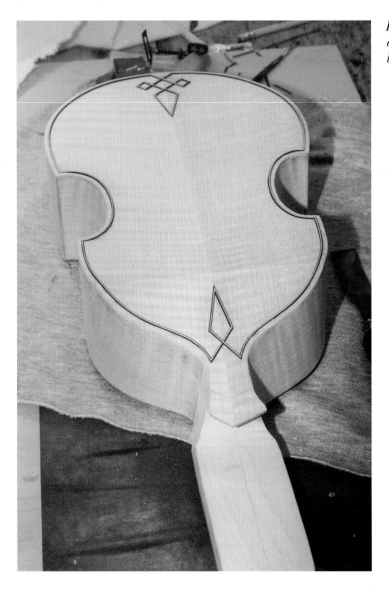

Fig. 153 All of the elements are fitted and glued, ready for levelling.

Fitting adjacent elements means confirming their mitred relationship. Symmetry and equality are possible only if identical joints are produced. Every effort must be concentrated on achieving this aim. If this means scrapping some parts, so be it. Purfling is not expensive, so overstock in case of accidents. It is best to complete a dry run with all elements fitted before any gluing.

It is best to use hot glue, for the simple reason that it may be reversed in case of the need to reposition or remove the purfling for any reason. It will probably be unnecessary to clamp the inlay or subject it to more pressure than the usual hammer treatment – pressing, not knocking, remember.

A freshly sharpened scraper should then be used to clean back the purfling and level the ground. What a blissful revelation!

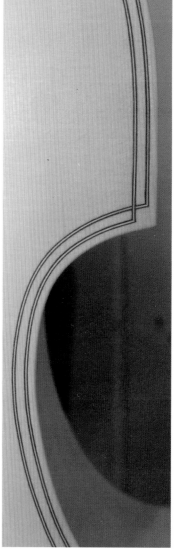

Fig. 154 A soundboard (front) with double purfling on a viol made by the great British luthier, Jane Julier.

(Right) *Fig. 155 Detail of the cross-over corners of the double purfling.*

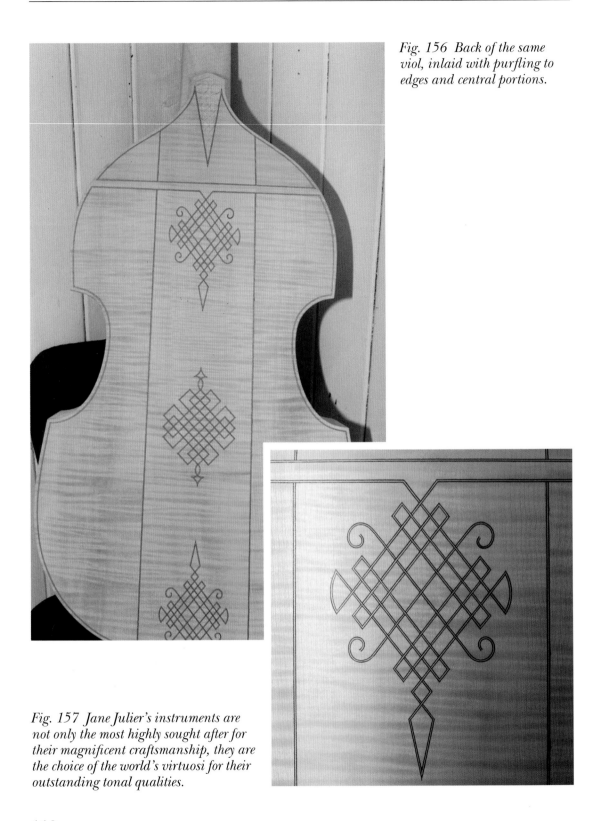

Fig. 156 Back of the same viol, inlaid with purfling to edges and central portions.

Fig. 157 Jane Julier's instruments are not only the most highly sought after for their magnificent craftsmanship, they are the choice of the world's virtuosi for their outstanding tonal qualities.

Creating an Inlay to Fit an Existing Recess

If an inlay is to be fitted into an existing recess, as in the case of a repair, it is a relatively easy process.

Normal procedure for decorating with inlay is almost always the making of the recess to suit the inlay element and it certainly makes more sense than the other way around. Occasionally, however, pieces become detached or damaged and need replacement. If the piece is old with a delicate patina, it is desirable to preserve the finish by taking extra care during the cleaning of the recess and the application of varnish after fitting the inlay, in the

Fig. 158 Two types of vernier calliper: the upper is made in plastic and gives direct readings of inner, outer and depth measurements. Plastic measuring devices are chosen for use on precious or fragile items. The lower version provides similar measuring features, but registers measurements on a dial gauge.

hope of disguising the repair. This work belongs to the specialist and is beyond the scope of this book, but for something of a domestic quality in need of an honest mend, this chapter should help.

PURFLING REPAIR

In the case of replacing a standard piece of purfling for a musical instrument repair, materials are available in abundance so these may be purchased. Likewise for the production of strings, etc., but again, if a small amount is needed, it is possible to produce some manually or by machine. Some careful trials to ascertain the width of the recess are all that should be required prior to the purchase of or the production of the stringing. A vernier calliper is ideal for measuring the width of the recess and the string.

If it is decided to make the string, whichever of several methods of production is used, it is essential after sawing (intentionally oversize) to trim the sides of the inlays to ensure its width is consistent. This may be achieved with the Wearing thicknesser, detailed in Chapter 2. The aim is to level and smooth the sides whilst at the same time thicknessing the inlay uniformly, the obvious sense of which needs no elaboration.

STRINGS FROM PURCHASED VENEER

Any veneer may be sliced into thin strips with a straight-edge and a sharp knife, with some discrete regard for grain direction and grain structure. To avoid cracking after slicing, the string should follow the direction of the run of the grain. It is perhaps obvious that to cut a slice across the grain will certainly result in a string that is destined to be broken. Cross-banding and inlays cut on the diagonal are specialized

products and not easily made by the home-craftsman. As to grain structure; best if the veneer is flat and smooth to avoid the need to straighten the piece after cutting.

It may be sufficient to place the straight-edge on the veneer at the correct position and apply a scalpel smartly to slice off the string. An experienced craftsman may do this with apparent ease. For the initiate, it is safer to hold the straight-edge in position with at least two clamps to obviate any movement during the cutting operation.

If the recess is curved to follow a shaped edge, as for a violin for example, it is best to match the radius of the string to the recess before attempting to fit it. This is to avoid breaking the relatively fragile string during the inlaying. The easiest way to achieve this is to damp the string with warm water and mould it around a heated former or by some

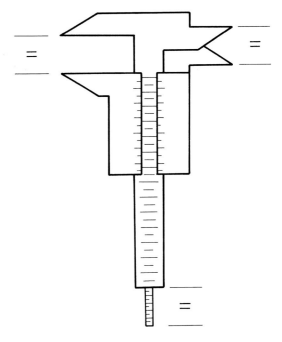

Fig. 159 Diagrammatic layout of a vernier calliper, illustrating its three functions: left-hand forks measure externally, right-hand forks measure internally and the protruding rod at the bottom measures depth.

similar means. A hair-drier may deliver sufficient heat for this purpose, or an electric fire, a cylinder heated by a gas flame, or what-have-you, will all be sufficient for this job. If the recess is curved in some complex fashion, it is probably best to create a mould of a similar shape to prepare the string prior to the fitting. Temporary attachment with tape to a mould until dry will provide a rigid element ready for embedding.

INLAYING THE STRING

Having prepared the string to the required shape and width, careful inspection of the recess should be made. This is best undertaken with a lens, since any irregularity will impede the process of embedding. Sometimes the channel may contain the remnants of the original glue, removal of which is essential. Thank your lucky stars if hot glue was used, since with hot water and patience it is possible to remove it easily. Alternative modern glues may give more problems.

If the sides are crumbly, as often happens with elderly pieces that have been in need of repair for any length of time, it may be necessary to 'clean back' the surface to reach solid material. This is best done after fitting the string, following which both ground and inlay are levelled simultaneously. Extra deep embedding may be necessary if the surface of the ground needs much cutting back.

Glue is added immediately before fitting, keeping at a minimum the time for the adhesive to soak into either the ground or the string. Should this happen, there is the likelihood of expansion occurring in one or both of the pieces, probably rendering difficulties in fitting. For similar reasons, leave plenty of time for the glue to harden before attempting to level the surface, otherwise tearing of the temporarily softened materials may occur due to the presence of unset glue.

Replacing a random or irregular-shaped motif is a different kind of problem.

REPLACING MOTIFS

The example shows a heart-shaped recess in a piece of sycamore. It was cut roughly and treated badly to emulate an existing, damaged, cavity. The procedure to create and fit a suitable motif is as follows:

Inspect the surface immediately surrounding the recess. If dents or defects have occurred to spoil the possibility of producing a clean edge joint between the recess and the motif, it may be necessary to recut the sides. A sharp knife, a keen eye and a steady hand are the order of the day. Assuming that either the edge was acceptable or that it has been corrected, choose a piece of suitable material for the motif. If other inlaid elements are present then these must be referred to, to help decide. Most usually, a material contrasting in colour is used.

Measure the depth of the recess with a vernier calliper and bring the inlay material

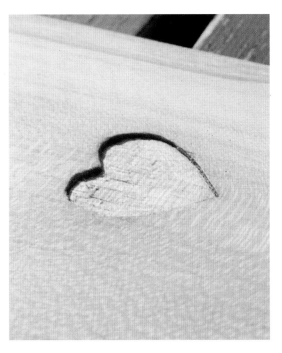

Fig. 160 A recess prepared for inlaying.

(Above) *Fig. 161 A soft crayon is used to trace on paper the outline of the recess.*

Fig. 162 After the preparation of the tracing, the paper is glued to the material chosen for the motif.

to suitable thickness. Best to make it slightly thicker for cleaning back after fitting.

Take a piece of thin paper and place it over the recess. Using a Chinagraph pencil or some other soft, waxy crayon, rub across the paper over the recess. This should define the shape of the recess, even to the detail of scars and blemishes.

Fix the paper pattern to the surface of the inlay material with adhesive and allow to set.

Cut out the motif using one of the following methods:

INCISING WITH A KNIFE

Beginning with gentle pressure following the marked line, increasing pressure progressively and repeating until the motif comes free. This takes care and patience, but it does work well.

TRIMMING WITH A ROUTER

With a fine rotary cutter driven by an inverted router mounted in a table designed for the purpose, it is possible to trim off surplus material leaving a clean line around the motif. The small Dremel Multi Tool may be combined with its own special attachment for this purpose, but care must be taken if the motif is small, since the operation means working relatively close to the rotating cutter.

CUTTING WITH A HAND FRETSAW OR POWERED SCROLLSAW

This is my own preference, particularly if it is a one-off, small item. The hand fretsaw is still used for the very finest of inlaid marquetry work and has every right to be considered alongside its younger relative, the powered scrollsaw.

If the saw-frame is held in contact with the arm, and the elbow acting as a pivot, a vertical reciprocation may be operated,

Fig. 163 An old-fashioned Hobbies fretsaw used for cutting out the motif. Notice the technique of resting the frame of the saw along the arm, raising and lowering whilst pivoting at the elbow to create the movement of a mechanical type.

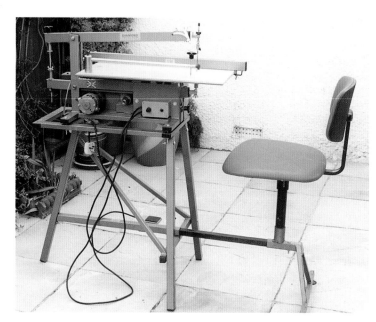

Fig. 164 An 'All systems go!', British made, Diamond machine scrollsaw by Douglas Woodward with every conceivable device to aid fast and precise sawing.

(Right) *Fig. 165 Blades as fine as sewing needles may be used with the scrollsaw.*

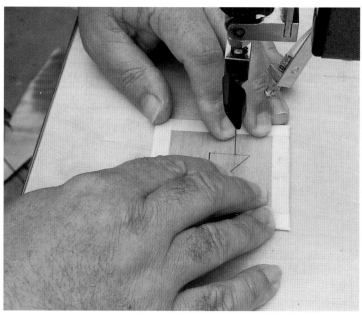

similar to that effected by machine scrollsaws. Or is it the other way around? A supplementary table with a V-notch cut in the front for saw access is fixed to the bench-top to give support to the workpiece during the sawing operation.

The machine scrollsaw performs the same task as the hand-held fretsaw but it oscillates much faster than the human arm and also with a controlled vertical movement. A professional model will cut from the thinnest veneers up to 100mm (4in) thick.

Fig. 166 Motif and recess ready for marriage.

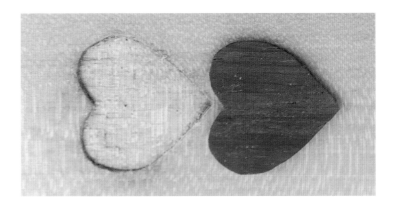

Some machines may also be slowed down to operate at speeds below 100 oscillations per minute and with fine blades may be used on very delicate work. The initial cost of a machine scrollsaw would be uneconomic if it were to be used by a hobbyist for infrequent inlaying projects, but the versatility of the machine allows many types of sawing operations in various materials, making it a versatile general purpose tool to own.

FITTING THE MOTIF

Assuming the motif has been cut out by whatever means, the paper may be removed. If it does not come off easily, no matter because the levelling process will clean it off. At least, the adhering paper will identify the top from the bottom ensuring its insertion the right way up.

A little scrape around the bottom corner will ensure there is no ragged edge to hinder

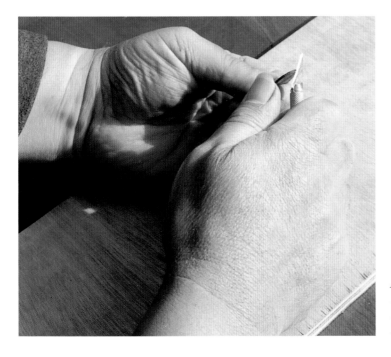

Fig. 167 Trimming the bottom corners to ensure an unimpeded embedding operation.

Fig. 168 Pressure with a clamp and pad during the gluing process.

its placing and a trial fit is made. If all is well, then it may be glued into position and clamped until dry. If all is not well, perhaps reference to the 'Troubleshooting' section in Chapter 14 will help.

(Below left) Fig. 169 Scraping off redundant surface material.

(Below) Fig. 170 A clean face with both motif and ground level ready for surface polish.

—20—

Adhesives

In the world of the woodworker, we have never had so much choice. However, modern adhesives lack the most important feature of the traditional, animal glues. It is not possible to reverse them. Oh, very well; some may be released with the introduction of an agent to soften the set adhesive, but the glue almost certainly cannot be reactivated and you may be sure you will have problems removing it from the wood in preparation for its replacement.

The old, 'hoof and hide', or concoctions made by boiling fish-bones, rabbit-skin, sinews, etc., are not only releasable, but may be reactivated and therefore re-usable just by the application of heat or hot water. Today such glue may be acquired from appropriate suppliers in granular form, requiring soaking in water to soften it.

Heating it will then create a mixture of glue and water, variable in consistency according to the liking of the user. It should be thin enough to apply to the joint with a brush somewhat like thin varnish.

In any kind of situation where separation is required of glued joints, animal glue has no superior. A happy alternative, mind you, particularly where small amounts are needed, is the Liquid Hide glue made by Franklins. It comes in a convenient bottle and needs no preparation other than to remove the top and tip it out. It is reversible and behaves very much like hot glue. Other more commonplace adhesives, such as Caseins, PVA, aliphatics, and epoxy resins, are well known and readily available at every hardware or woodwork store.

Fig. 171 An example of wide stringing used to enhance an otherwise pedestrian picture frame. Tunbridge-ware inlays like this are produced by William Adams.

— 21 —

The Finish

This final chapter title was deliberately chosen for its double-meaning, as shall be readily understood.

The term used to describe the way in which a surface is finally treated is called 'the finish'. It is one of those subjects that may be given endless treatment and fill volumes, and it has. Students may enjoy some further research on the subject to get the best out of their materials and projects. For now – given that the normal excellent smooth and level surface has been prepared, without scratches and scuffs – try the following quick, easy, and sure way to a respectable foolproof finish!

Acquire one of the following: Tru-oil, Danish oil, Teak oil or something similar. Plain linseed will do at a pinch, but the ones mentioned are better.

With a soft cloth or brush, give a generous application of oil to the surface, working well into the grain and removing any surplus with a wipe-over with a soft dry cloth. Let it dry and admire the effect of the oil.

Rub down the dried, oiled, surface, using either very fine abrasive papers or the finest wire wool. Apply several more coats of the oil, drying and rubbing down in between. Take a proprietary wax polish, preferably beeswax-based coming semi-solid in tins. Use a clean cloth or even a new piece of wire wool and rub over the surface lightly with wax polish. Buff it up immediately with another clean cloth to make a soft sheen. More wax and more burnishing may be applied to give a deeper gloss if required.

Now you can stand back and reflect on, and in, your beautiful work.

Fig. 172 Turned objects with inlaid William Adams Tunbridge-ware stringing, embedded in channels produced during the turning operation whilst still mounted on the lathe.

Glossary

Banding or binding A plain, single or multiple strip for inlaying, usually into a corner rebate.

Baryton A member of the viol family with six strings for bowing and sixteen sympathetic strings. Its pitch range categorized it as a bass, or baritone, instrument.

Bench-dogs Square or cylindrical posts, about a hand's-width in length and about as thick as a thumb. Normally used in pairs or multiples of two, to act as clamps. A row of holes in a row along a bench-top would be aligned with one in the movable vice-jaw. Thus, a work-piece could be held between the dog in the moving vice-jaw and one inserted in a bench hole.

Bending iron Usually made not of iron, but of steel pipe or an alloy casting; the latter shaped for a specific purpose. A source of heat is applied to raise the temperature of the metal to permit wooden strips or bands to be softened and reformed.

Burnisher, or 'ticketer' A tool similar to a small butcher's steel for sharpening knives, but in this case used for turning over the edges of scraper blades to create a burr.

Circle-cutter Used for marking or cutting circular lines. A blade is fitted into a cross shaft, adjustable to and from a central point used as a pivot, similar in principle to a pair of compasses.

Collet pencil A propelling pencil, whose lead may be advanced progressively and gripped mechanically with a collet.

Cutting gauge The more correct, but less used, name given to the tool usually called the 'purfling cutter'. It is used for marking or incising a line parallel to an edge or corner. It may be used for marking across the grain.

Ditching Used to describe the delineation of the periphery of a 'field', or recess, by channelling in preparation for the clearing of the inner waste from its floor.

Fence A guide, or bearing, against which a work-piece or other material may be leant for repetitive actions, or to produce a parallel reference for cutting or other operations.

Fishtail chisel So-called because of its appearance, being wider at its cutting edge than in the shank.

Fretsaw Traditional name for what is now more commonly called a scrollsaw. There is the tendency to call the manual variety by the former name, the machine type by the latter.

Frondose A picturesque term used to describe designs suggested by foliage.

Ground The item or material into which an inlay is to be embedded.

Hand-router Its main feature is a cut-adjustable, cranked cutter which is used to chisel out waste.

Hold-down, or hold-fast A clamp with a vertical action to hold work down on a bench-top. Its pillar is fitted into a hole in the bench creating a locking action by a slight tilt, when pressure is exerted onto the work by its screw action.

Line Or band, or string. Usually square in section, a plain, one-colour material and at the lower end of the size range.

Lutherie From the old term meaning literally 'lute-making'; now taken to mean the making of any type of musical instrument.

MDF The recognised abbreviation for medium-density fibreboard; developed in the USA, by binding together timber fibres with resin, then rolling, pressing and cutting to size.

Marking gauge Similar to a cutting gauge but with a sharp pin rather than a blade. Not advised for cross-grain marking, due to the risk of tearing.

Marquetry The cutting and gluing side-by-side of decorative wood, usually from veneers. Usually, the natural characteristics of the grain, texture and colour are employed to create a pictorial effect.

Mitre guide Fixed at useful angles, such as 30, 45 or 60 degrees, this is used similarly to a set-square to establish mitre joints.

Mortise A recess made to correspond to a tenon (qv). The two parts are brought together, one in each of two parts, to create a joint.

Motif A distinctive idea or theme elaborated into a shape or form as a design.

Odd-legs Made from a pair of divider callipers with legs of unequal length. The end of each leg is ground to a knife point to permit marking or incising. The point of the longer leg is inserted into an existing incision which is used as a guide. As it is traversing, the point of the shorter leg marks or incises a parallel line to the original.

Purfling The type of string or band inlay associated with musical instruments; consisting of a central strip contrasting in colour with the two outer strips.

Purfling cutter Incorrectly-named tool used for marking or incising channels to receive purfling and not, as its name suggests, to cut purfling.

Rebate A recess along the edge of a ground or work-piece to form a channel to receive an inlaid part. Its original term was 'rabbet'.

Rebec A small fiddle, Arabic in origin whose body is shaped like an elongated half-pear, carved from one piece of wood.

Renaissance The period marking the waning of the Middle Ages and the rise of the modern world. Generally taken to be around the fourteenth century.

Rosette A circular arrangement of wooden ribbons or strips enclosing a Tunbridge ware (qv) pattern of geometrical forms.

Router A portable power tool with an in-built electric motor to drive cutters of the rotary type, used for plunge-boring or side cutting to produce channels. It may be used freehand, with accessories or attached to a table.

Scratch-stock Used to cut grooves or to work mouldings. Made in the workshop to individual requirements; consisting of two pieces of wood shaped like an inverted 'L', clamped with screws to hold the cutter. It may be used to cut 'stopped' grooves and also to follow curved edges.

Scrollsaw A motorized saw with a reciprocating vertical movement carrying a fine blade for the cutting of motifs and other delicate items.

Seam-roller A roller, wood or plastic, with a metal spindle held between the forks of a wooden handle, to roll out joins in paper or any other situation where point pressure is required, uniformly, over a large area.

Secretaire A writing bureau with storage for stationery and writing materials. French in style, as the name suggests.

Shaker A name given to an offshoot of the Quaker sect, noted for their unadorned, functional, furniture and utilitarian artefacts.

Shoulder knife A knife with a handle long enough to be rested on the shoulder to provide control whilst incising recesses.

Sliding bevel For testing or marking unusual angles. Its blade is adjustable for angle and length and fixed temporarily with a thumb-screw.

String, see stringing.

Stringing An inlay of either plain or decorative wood, sometimes called banding, made of either one single piece or multiple strips.

Tenon The projecting part in one member made to match the mortise (qv) in another, to enable the joining of the two.

Thicknesser, Stringing A special tool comprising a blade, its holder and a table. The blade position over the table is adjustable for height, permitting the setting of a gap through which banding or other slender materials may be passed to regulate the uniformity of their thickness.

Ticketer, *see* burnisher.

Toothpick chisel So-called because of its small size. A cranked blade of steel, usually made by the user from a nail, inserted into a wooden handle.

Tunbridge-ware A form of miniature marquetry associated with the town of Tunbridge Wells, Kent. Square sectioned strips, of carefully chosen colour, are glued together to form patterns, similar to 'Blackpool Rock' and sliced across into thin tiles. When laid side by side, these tiles may be formed into further designs. The finest designs form entire pictorial motifs.

Veneer A thin slice of wood, chosen for its fine appearance and intended to be glued to a material of inferior quality. Cut either by saw or knife to thicknesses as little as 0.6mm (0.025in).

Veneer hammer Intended not for hammering but for applying local pressure in a stroking operation across veneer during the gluing stage. It consists of a handle set into a wooden stock fitted with a brass strip, for contact with the veneered surface.

Vernier calliper A precision measuring device incorporating the facility to measure three dimensions: internal, external and depth.

Wonder dog A variation on the 'bench' dog (qv), in that it utilizes the holes in the bench top to locate its pillar to act as an anchor. Pressure is then applied by its screw to clamp a workpiece between its jaw and a normal bench dog.

Index

American black walnut 39
Arkansas 43

Banding 35, 57
Bench grinder 43
Bench stone 44
Bending iron 79
Bevel, blade 44, 45
Binding 35
Boxes 33, 34
Brazilian Rosewood 89
British Museum 12
Brushes 21
Burring a scraper 49–54
Byzantine 9

Carborundum grit 43
Celtic knot 105
Channelling 69–74
Chinagraph pencil 116
Chisels 13, 83, 85
Circle-cutter 16, 101–3
Clamps 26
Colour-dying 40
Corner banding 57–68
Crawford, Andrew 33, 34
Cutting gauge 57–68, 77

Dark Ages 9
Diamond scrollsaw 118
Dremel 21, 61–3, 73–74, 89–91

Ebony 39–40
Egyptians 9
Electric router 30
Excavation, principles of 81–8

Fingerboard, decorated 42, 99, 100
Fire, protection against 31
Fretsaw 21, 117

Gothic 10
Gouges 13
Greco–Roman symbols 40
Grounds, types of 33
Guitar 41, 42, 101–4

Hand-router 16, 17, 95, 103–4
Heating 30
Holly 39, 40
Holtey, Carl 14–15, 18–19, 55, 77, 97
Hone 43

Inlay, types of 35
Inlaying an existing recess 113–19
Irregular shapes, inlaying 92
Italy 10

Julier, Jane 111–12

Knife 14–15, 44–5, 77–8, 82, 93–4

Leather 43
Lighting 29
Lines 36, 98–9
Lute 42, 99–100
Lutherie 10
Luthier 36

MacDonald router attachment 61–3
MacDonald router base 89–91
Maggini violin 37
Magnifying lens 26

Mahogany 40
Marking gauge 26
Marquetry 36–7
MDF 34, 43
Mitre guide 76
Mock-shading 38, 39
Moorish knot 105
Mosaic 10
Mother-of-pearl 42
Motifs 36, 37, 38, 39, 40, 93–8, 115–20
Motorized router 19
Motorized scrollsaw 22, 30, 117–18

Odd-leg dividers 22, 23, 107

Panel, inlaying 81–8
Plane 18
Planing 58
Powered abrasives 30
Purfling 35, 36, 41, 42, 105–12
Purfling cutter 14, 46, 55, 69–70
Purfling jig 73–4
Purfling repair 114

Renaissance 10
Rosette 36, 40, 101–4
Rotary veneer cutter 11

Safety at work 31
Scalpel 43
Scraper 17–18, 48–54, 80, 92, 120
Scraper-plane 18, 20
Scratch-stock 17, 65–8, 98
Scrollsaw 22, 30
Seam-roller 25
Secretaire 12

Set-square 25
Shaker 11
Shaping inlays, tools for 22
Sharpening 43, 46–8
Sharpening apparatus 26, 46–7
Shoulder knife 10
Slate 43
Sliding bevel 25
Steel straight-edge 25
Storage 31
Stringing 35, 65–80, 114–15
Stringing, curved 77–80
Stringing-thicknesser 22–4

Thicknessing 22–4
Ticketer 48
Toothpick chisel 13, 78, 96
Tortoiseshell 42
Trimming motifs 117
Troubleshooting, in excavation 88
Tunbridge-ware 36

Vacuum cleaners 31
Veneer 10
Veneer hammer 25
Veritas 28
Vernier calliper 113–14
Viol 105–12

Walnut 40
Water stone 43
Wearing, Bob 22
Wood-colour 39
Work-bench 27
Workshop 27